BEBE & FRIENDS

Tails of Rescue

Jean Rodenbough

ALL THINGS
THAT
MATTER
PRESS

Jean Rodenbough

BEBE & FRIENDS
Tails of Rescue
Copyright © 2012 by Jean Rodenbough

ISBN: 978-0-9885427-3-0

Library of Congress Control Number: 2012955069

Cover design by All Things That Matter Press

Published in 2012

In Memorium

BESS

1997-2012

Acknowledgments

Where do I begin to acknowledge all those to whom I am indebted for contributing to this book! They shared their stories and photos about beloved pets with little to receive from their efforts but a copy of this book and the satisfaction of having told important stories. That they took time out of their busy lives to share the great love possible between human beings and the animal world is a gift for all of us.

I am also grateful for the work of thousands of rescue organizations across the nation whose dedication provides shelter and all that is necessary for animals under their care. Large organizations, such as the ASPCA® and The Humane Society of the US, not only advocate and act in the interest of all creatures, but provide educational opportunities about what constitutes good care for them. It has been the hard work of all organizations and rescue groups, in partnership with committed individuals, to insist upon laws protecting animal life, both wild and domestic. The public has been informed and, in turn, many have joined various organizations that advocate proper treatment of animals.

Others I am grateful to are those who have critiqued the poems, proof-read the raw copy, made helpful suggestions, prepared the photo collection, and in a myriad of other ways helped with this book. It would not have made the full journey to publication without them. Among those is my editor at All Things That Matter Press, Deb Harris, who provided solace, wisdom, and encouragement along with her editorial advice. Some with artistic skills made the pages come into focus and meaning. Our daughter Kit Rodenbough spent hours preparing print-ready photographs of the rescues pictured here, in addition to her many responsibilities with her vintage business. Her own rescue Chihuahua, Bebe, contributed her likeness, along with other rescues. Grace the Yellow Dog brought the endeavor full circle by leading readers from beginning to end. Our four children, and later their own families, have taken in many dogs and cats over the years: rescues, fosters, and those of pure lineage. I must also include several goldfish, turtles, mice, a parakeet, and a rabbit. We are a family who from the beginning has made homes for our companions, the ones who taught us much about their animal kingdom.

It is important also to acknowledge the contributions of all the animals whose stories are included here. They give, and have given, of their willingness to be partners in life with their human companions, often in spite of mistreatment and ignorance which brought them harm. Great and small, they are our companions on the journey. They are blessings to the world.

Table of Contents

A Sense of Something

We know . . .
as if communication were not only by words,
we know there is something
we can never fully know: that our animal spirit
lives through the lives of those un-humans
who seek to tell us who they are. We know.

Introduction

Collecting stories of animals who have been abused, neglected, and unwanted is a difficult endeavor. When I first got the idea of putting together a collection of stories about how these wonderful creatures eventually found loving and caring homes, I envisioned it would be an interesting and easy task. All I had to do was get in touch with rescue organizations for information, ask all my friends to contribute their stories, put requests on Twitter and Facebook and anywhere else that might bring forth accounts of taking in a dog or cat or other non-human creature. I had published a book just recently using a similar format, with stories about those who were children during the Second World War. That volume came together in a reasonable amount of time.

To my surprise, even with my experience of working with such a format, the challenge in preparing this book has been daunting. One difficulty developed in reading through the stories that came to me, along with photographs of these much loved pets. Each account had its wonderful aspects, but each one also tore at my heart. I could work for only short periods of time on the book before feeling overwhelmed and I would have to put the project aside for a time. The stories lingered, however, as I worked with them. I followed information on websites of animal rescue organizations. I dwelt on newspaper articles about animal hoarders and puppy mills. My overriding compulsion became to make those abused lives memorable by honoring all creatures. Perhaps by doing so, by making public their stories, I could find some peace.

These stories describe how the lives of some animals—whether from shelters public streets, cages, or hiding from the known and unknown dangers stalking them—were changed, their ability to trust finally developed when they found safe homes and loving caregivers and companion animals.

The regret, of course, is that not all such lives were changed, nor did all stories end happily. Eventually, our animal friends described here must meet the last days of their too brief lives. My hope is that more and more will do so within a caring and loving environment, surrounded by their beloved humans. The call weighs heavily upon each of us to work for such a goal.

Included here along with the stories are photographs when available and information about organizations that serve as rescuers or as shelters for animals brought to them. The statistics are as current as I could locate, but whatever numbers are listed may have increased. Also noted in this book are a few statistics about pets, stray animals, shelters, and rates of adoption, as well as information about euthanasia for animals, related mostly to dogs and cats. Some rescue organizations, in addition to the usual pets taken in, can handle larger animals such as horses, goats, sheep, and, in some cases, cows and other farm animals.

As for those who contributed stories, their names and locations are included. My deep gratitude goes out to each one for taking the time to join me in this endeavor. Thank you.

~Jean Rodenbough

4

nothing daunts her search
for family, food, friendship
or a scratch
behind the ears
intrepid in her dogship
she engages us
without conditions
no barriers between
what is lost or found
when with a swing
of her powerful tail
she gathers us in that sweep
shares her joie de vivre
contagious and freely offered
defines grace in shades of gold

Grace will be our guide through these pages.

Let me welcome you to this collection of stories about us—I mean those of us who have had terrible lives until the Right Person came along to give us homes of love and care. I am one of those. My first seven years were spent in a cage, and I never knew about grass or creeks or running with other dogs and being with those two-legged animals you call humans. I did know the difference between daylight and dark, though. There were others like me, lined up in cages, row on row, never able to sniff one another or communicate nose to nose.

Let me take back that last part. Every few months another dog almost like me was put in my cage with me and did awful things to me. A few months later a whole bunch of little dogs that looked like me came out of my belly and stayed with me a while. I grew to love them very much. Then suddenly one day hands reached in and took them all away from me. This story happened over and over to me until I became sick and I hurt all over. I think my days were getting short. It was then that something good happened to me, and to all of my fellow cagers: more humans came and took us away from that place of unhappiness. Now I live with my wonderful MamaKit, who loves me and takes me to a doctor who has given me health and a new life.

Anyone who sees me might think there is still something wrong with me. I had some operations. My teeth are all gone and my tongue hangs out. I am afraid of lots of sounds and people. But MamaKit holds me when I get scared. I love her very much. Especially when she takes me on walks through a place with grass and a creek along with the other dogs who live at our house.

In this book you will read about animals who have had a bad time in their lives until they, too, were given new homes with people who love them. They are happy now, but sometimes they think about those bad days. I don't know the ones you will read about, but they are special. So here's to all of us who have found love and happiness. Maybe you will find one of us who needs a good home and someone to love who gives care and love in return.

Misty & Rocky

Contributed by **Sandra Barnes**, Greensboro, North Carolina

Many years ago, about six months after I lost a mixed-breed terrier, who was a rescue, my vet called me about two Yorkshire Terriers in an abusive situation. Would I be willing to take them in?

I hesitated at first, because I preferred taking only one dog, but was willing to visit those two. Apparently, they had been together since birth and depended upon each other. It was necessary for them to stay together.

We agreed on a time for me to visit the dogs, who lived with a couple involved in a contentious relationship. The man was extremely abusive of their three dogs, and his wife feared that he would kill them. She planned to take the mother of the two pups and leave, but could not take the other two with her. The result: those two little ones came home with me! Misty settled in quickly, but her brother Rocky took longer to adjust to the change. He remained forever afraid of men. My husband was the only man who could get near him. In response to others, if they moved toward him quickly, he'd throw himself to the floor and scream in terror. Despite his fears and his fragile frame, he turned out to be full of heart and determination.

Misty was the one who served as "protector." Whenever we were out walking and someone approached, she would put her entire ten pounds between me and the other person, bare her teeth, and growl. Such ferocity from a tiny animal! Sad to note, Misty's heart failed her when she was nine, and no attempts could save her. Her death left Rocky completely bereft. He stopped eating and playing and just cried and moped around. When we brought another rescued dog in to keep him company, he hated her. After a week of his screaming and carrying on, we finally took the new dog back to her former shelter.

From that time on, Rocky took over the household. We could almost hear him say, "I want to be an only child!" Once again he began eating, playing, and showing his happiness.

Rocky remained our star dog until his kidneys failed at sixteen. But we knew that for as long as those two lived with us, not only had they brought gifts of joy to us, we had brought happiness and peace to these two beautiful little dogs.

10

Winnie

Contributed by **Lynda Baker-Sheffer**, Fort Defiance, Virginia

When I worked at Oak Ridge Military Academy near Greensboro, North Carolina, my son Scott would spend his summer mornings picking tobacco for the football coach at the school. Later in the day this unlikely duo—a very small ten-year-old boy and a larger than life senior citizen—would head off to play pool, go catfishing, or visit the locals. One such afternoon, "Coach" took Scott to visit a local breeder who also had a small plot of tobacco that needed to be picked. The pay was exceptional, especially in the eyes of a small boy whose mother was struggling financially following the sudden death of his father.

On Friday afternoon Scott went to collect his week's wages. Much to his delight, the owner asked, "Would you rather have cash … or a puppy?" This breeder of championship Chows had a "runt" in his last litter that would have to be destroyed because she didn't "measure up." The last thing I needed was another mouth to feed, but I agreed to go see the pup. Common wisdom is that you're not supposed to pick the single most rambunctious pup in the pen, nor the most docile.

I looked over the beautiful balls of fur and there she was. She sat a little ways off, watching her little mates bouncing in one big pile. We made eye contact. Then she calmly got up and walked over to the fence and stuck her paw through the opening, as if to shake my hand, and smiled. Yes. She smiled and that was it.

We got her the spring that my daughter April turned three. "Winnie!" April squealed with delight. So "Winnie" she was.

She was immediately potty-trained, never chewed a single shoe, or barked inappropriately. She loved to travel, stand guard over child or cat, and in time became an affectionate and caring mother of three black Lab babies. She knew the boundaries of our yard and saw to it that we were not invaded by unwanted visitors. She slept by my bed that first night and every night thereafter. Winnie was the color of spring honey and just as sweet. She played with children of all ages and politely shook hands at the slightest opportunity. Once we were camping in the National Forest.

Gary, my husband, and April had gone to collect firewood and Winnie had stayed behind with me. I heard her give a yip and turned to look. She had kicked up a flock of small yellow butterflies and was bouncing joyfully with them. It was a vision out of *Paradise Lost*.

Now, years after her passing, I still remember that warm summer afternoon and her sheer joy at being part of the universe.

Winnie taught us that size doesn't matter when your heart is open, and that there is always room for one more at the table.

Cinderella

Contributed by **Suzanne Herzing,** Mission, Texas
www.cinderella-pet-rescue.org

Cinderella is a Daschund named for the Cinderella Pet Rescue Organization where she was taken for shelter after being rescued. She had been abandoned along with her five pups, and was found in a pasture trying to keep her litter fed but hidden from view. She had managed to do so in spite of bad weather and a dangerous environment. She bravely guarded the pups against potential attackers, but had suffered some wounds, as had two of the pups. Even so, it took several attempts to get them all to safety. Once at the shelter, "Cindy" was able to realize that the staff was there to help her. With a steady supply of food and water at her disposal, they soon began to see what a wonderful dog she was. She flourished under their care, loved to be around people and other dogs, and even got along with the cats! She is now living on a farm with a loving family, taking many trips with them, and enjoying a happy life.

The claim of the staff at Cinderella Pet Rescue has become reality for Cindy and others they rescue: "We make hairy-tail fairy-tales come true!"

13

Perhaps some of Cinderella's relatives!

Many of the stories here describe rescued animals who at some point were cared for at animal shelters. Information gathered by such organizations as the ASPCA® and The Humane Society of the United States will provide a picture of how many of the shelters now operate in this country. At this time, there is no official set of statistics on animal rescues or other efforts to protect animals. Estimates, however, are considered to be a general reflection of what is being done to in those areas.

Each year, somewhere between six and eight million companion animals are in the approximately five thousand animal shelters in communities across the United States. How did they end up in shelters? About half were picked up by an animal control unit and half were relinquished by their owners. Of these, three to four million, or sixty percent of the dogs and seventy percent of the cats, end up being euthanized because of space limits, incurable health issues, and limited adoption. Only a very small number, about two percent, are returned to owners, mostly because of IDs of some sort.

An interesting fact is that over twenty percent of people who leave their dogs in a shelter had previously adopted them from one. Various reasons cause them to return the dogs.

As far as other ways that pets find homes, it is estimated that most pet owners receive their animals from family members and friends as gifts. About thirty eight percent of pet owners purchase their pets from breeders or pet stores. Approximately ten to twenty percent of household pets come from shelters and rescues. These animals as a whole are found in about sixty-three percent of American households, constituting some seventy-five million dogs and about eighty-five million cats. Of these, about seventy-five percent are neutered, in contrast to only ten percent of the animals received by shelters.

The time limit for holding animals in a shelter varies,

depending on available space, as well as the health and temperament of the individual animal. Sadly, some simply are not good candidates for adoption. In many cases, state or local laws determine the required holding period for strays, the usual being five days including a weekend day. If severe illness or behavioral problems exist that require treatment or training beyond the capability of a shelter, euthanasia may be recommended. Some animal shelters are operated as no-kill shelters—and all animal welfare organizations would prefer such a policy. Such locations require strong public support, financially and otherwise, in order to operate within an expanded budget and additional professional care for the animals. Statistics on animal rescues and protection are currently not tabulated nationally by any government institution or animal organization. It is possible to find other resources, however. Some of those are the National Council on Pet Population Study & Policy, the American Veterinary Medical Association, and the American Pet Products Manufacturers Association. The latter is a good resource for statistics on pets and pet ownership in this country. Their website provides current information: http://www.appma.org/pubs_survey.asp.

Other websites include alleycat.org, feralcat.com, nhes.org, and spayusa.org.

a place away from the noise
away from biting cold
the fear of what is known –
someone cares enough
makes space and company
for others like this one
brought into safety and the gift
of food after hungry days
distrust is long in fading even
here among the others
and now the wait
for what comes next

Bubu

Contributed by **Andy Gwynn**, Black Mountain, North Carolina

Bubu chose us. She showed up at the house eight years ago in the spring: a small, scared puppy. We assume she was born nearby. I don't know why she chose us; that will always be a mystery. But we fell for her from the start. She was just a dog, a mixed breed of uncertain origin and lineage. The best kind.

To our great consternation, one thing she loved to do was occasionally roll around in something really foul-smelling. And she was probably the world's worst watchdog. She would run up into the woods and hide if a strange car drove up.

Despite these small failings, she was our dog and she was the best. She was sweet through and through. She loved kids and possessed a goofy and comical spirit. Even though she was very well-trained and behaved, there was always just a touch of her elemental wild nature there. I often said the reason she was sent to us was to make us laugh. She essentially lived free, like a dog should, and she stayed around close by without being tethered to a leash or fenced in. She knew where her home was.

She loved to go "rabbit hunting" in the woods with her buddy Chewy. Once she even caught one! Mostly it was just good exercise — for her and the rabbits, too.

The end for Bubu came too soon for us who loved her so, but she knew it was time. She was my daughter Eme's dog above all, although she was loyal to all of her human family. In her last days it was a struggle for her just to get up, but she would climb the stairs every night during the night to sleep outside of Eme's room. Last night Eme brought a pad and her covers downstairs and slept beside her on the floor so Bu wouldn't have to make that difficult trip up.

I write this on the morning that our Bubu died. We knew she had been failing in the last few days. I took her outside for a bathroom break and we had just come inside. It was clear that the time for the difficult decision was at hand. I was on the phone making arrangements to get a vet to come to the house to put her down when I noticed she wasn't breathing. I got down on the floor and held her and talked to her as she took her last couple of ragged breaths. It was complete and peaceful—the way it should be.

I called Eme and she came home from school. We dug a grave in the woods on the east side of the house where Bu liked to lie in the sun. Then we mourned her passing and celebrated her life.

It happens to be Holy Week on the church calendar as I am writing this. I can't help but notice the congruency of burials. While I don't expect to see Bu walking along the road to Emmaus, I am confident that she will indeed be resurrected as her mortal remains cycle through the roots of the trees, plants, and flowers that will cover her. From old life comes new life.

I'm going to miss this old dog. For thirty-two years now, I have not lived without a dog. Matter of fact, most all of my life I've lived in the company of one dog or another. I'm sure there will be another somewhere down the road. But not right now.

Bubu was born on North Fork, lived her days on North Fork, and died on North Fork There she will remain. And, of course, she will remain always in our hearts.

Vacant

in a corner of the room lies an old ball
its cover frayed by use
and dried dog drool
a pet's bed against the wall, rolled up
now unused

we forget so much about who was here
who has gone on
the silence of that absence
speaks the story

21

Sophie Marie

Contributed by **Carol Gillentine**, Greensboro, North Carolina

My friend said, "Get a dog, it'll keep you from becoming hard." I was recovering from a knee replacement and needed a new hip. I now lived with my daughter, a situation which had turned out to be a blessing. My long time relationship had ended a few months earlier; so much for the bliss that comes with retirement. Since I am a dog lover, the advice seemed like a good idea. I headed for the animal shelter.

All the dogs were too young and energetic, but as my eyes became accustomed to the dim light at the shelter I saw a big blob of fur sleeping in the corner of the cage. They brought her outside to me and, even with the fur, she was very heavy—she had a "shelf" on her backside. She looked like a miniature Chow, but she was part Pomeranian and something. I immediately felt very loved although she did not physically show it. She had been at the shelter for thirty days. She was older. The shelter person guessed her age to be six or seven, but I knew better—more like nine or ten.

Our first stop was my vet's, where they estimated her age at ten or eleven and healthy, but overweight by twenty-five pounds. Then we were off to the groomer's for the "everything" she needed. When I picked her up she looked like a Sophia Maria, but mostly Sophie Marie. We walked into the house, and she immediately curled up in the bed I had for her. She looked up at me, her big cataract-covered eyes filled with love and gratitude.

There is no doubt in my mind that animals are very aware of kindness and love. Her favorite place eventually became my recliner atop me and her blanket.

It took a while to break her from eating acorns when she was in our back yard. I suspect that may have been what she ate before she was picked up. She was housebroken and would bark to get out. And she found out early on that my daughter would feed her from the table. She would get in line with Max and Odie, our other pets, for her share. She would also plant herself right next to me wherever I was in the house, as though I were the most important person in the world and she had to be with me. When I talked to her, she would cock her head from one side to the other.

One thing that happens when persons are grieving a loss is the need to tell their story *many* times, and Sophie would listen to mine as if it were the first time every time. After a while I didn't need to tell the story as often, but we talked about many other things.

I tell her that we "old girls" move slower and have problems hearing and seeing—and our joints hurt—but we still have a lot of life left in us. Since I brought her home two years ago, I've had shoulder surgery, back surgery, and a hip replacement. Sophie has been my constant companion. And now she is having her own hip problem. We understand these things, and help each other.

I think of what my friend said about "becoming hard." He was right. In fact, having Sophie in my life has made for an even softer me.

Snowball

Contributed by **Melanie Rodenbough**, Greensboro, North Carolina

Eighteen years ago I took my two young daughters, ages eight and five, to a Pet Adoption Fair at the pet store at the Lawndale Shopping Center. And, of course, we came home with two kittens: a very shy tabby who had been mistreated and a very sociable white kitten who had been bottle fed from an early age.

While it took a while for "Socks" to become acclimated to our family, "Snowball" was immediately comfortable and compliant with being dressed, riding in a doll carriage, and a variety of other little girl play.

Within the first year, however, "Snowy" developed a tumor on his hind foot, and ultimately we had to make the decision whether to put him to sleep, send him off for very expensive radiation treatment that might not work, or remove the whole leg. The first option was not even considered.

The day he came home from his surgery, he walked out of the kennel on three legs, headed for the litter box and the water bowl, and never looked back.

He has outlasted his buddy Socks, as well as two other cats and three dogs, and continues to reign supreme in our house.

In his old age he loves a variety of soft places at floor level, but still climbs the stairs every morning to meow outside our bedroom door when he's ready for breakfast. Two serious health problems— a thyroid condition that required radiation treatment, and surgery to remove a non-cancerous tumor on his back—did nothing to interrupt his equanimity.

One of my daughters once placed a paper red heart on Snowy, a fitting emblem for a cat who has been such a love. He is always

25

happy, always ready to "talk" to anyone who will pay him attention, and always happy to lick his human friends. And lick. And lick some more ....

Radar

An Autobiographical Tail

(Note: although the rescuer shared this story, Radar wanted to tell it his way. So here is his own version of how he came to live with his people, **Cathy and Frank Lundblad**, *Raleigh, North Carolina.)*

I can't tell you a whole lot about my life before I came to a good home. I remember a road, and I was afraid to go across it because there were loud and fast machines that smelled like they could mean danger. I had enough danger in my life already, in a place where two-leggeds yelled at me and hit me and took me from my mother and my brothers and sisters. I ran away.

If life had been hard for me before, it was terrible then. I didn't know where I was, and I was outside where things would bite me. My people now tell me these were ticks and fleas all over me. I was miserable and hungry and thirsty. They told me one of my dew claws was really bad. No wonder it hurt so much.

So there I was, beside that road where loud and fast things went by, and I was hurting and scratching and afraid—and I was just a little pup.

Then I saw one of those big machines on the road stop and a two-legged got out of it and stood looking at me. I looked back, afraid I'd get hit or yelled at again for running away. Instead, she talked to me real softly, and invited me to get into that big loud machine. I was scared, but whatever happened to me couldn't be worse than what I had been through, so I took the chance and went with her.

She took me to a place that smelled clean, where there were more two-leggeds who took care of me for a few days. They told me they were looking for the people who owned me. I was hoping they'd never find out—and they didn't. These nice two-leggeds took care of my sore dew claw, gave me good food, then put me in a big tub of water and got rid of those awful things that had been biting me. I felt so good at last!

By this time they had given me a name. It wasn't one that I had before, but there wasn't any way to tell them that because I didn't have a collar or anything with my name on it. They looked at my big ears that stood out from me real straight and started calling me Radar. That's been my name ever since.

One day not long after I began to feel much better, I went to a place where the people—the ones I used to call two-leggeds—said I could stay with them until I got all the way well again. Then maybe someone would give me a home for good. While I was with these people, I learned some manners and what it was like to trust humans. They never yelled at me or hit me. Sometimes they might scold me if I did something they didn't like, but I learned not to do whatever it was that they didn't like again.

I wondered who the people were who might give me a for-keeps home. I waited. And I waited. Then the people who took me in sat down beside me and said they'd like for me to live with them all the time, if I would like that. I jumped up and wagged my tail, to let them know that was really what I wanted all the time!

I'm now as big as I'll get, and I am so happy. I've almost forgotten those bad times from when I was little. I hope no other animal has to go through what I did. I have found a place with a lot of love for me and I give it back to my people every chance I get.

Animal Rescue & Foster Program

This rescue-foster program has been operating since 1992 under a 501(c)(3) not-for-profit status, as a charitable organization. Funding is solely through membership and private donations, with no funding from governmental bodies of the state, county, or City of Greensboro, North Carolina, where it is located. Opened in 2002, ARFP's Next Step Adoption Center is the largest no-kill adoption center in the area and houses more than ten to fifteen felines full time.

Dedicated to finding homes for abandoned puppies and kittens, ARFP provides foster and medical care prior to placing them in adoptive homes with responsible caregivers. All adopted pets are spayed or neutered as a step in decreasing overpopulation of unwanted animals.

Among the programs offered are adoptive services, foster care by ARFP volunteers, rescue resources when foster homes are unavailable, medical care including vaccinations and preventive treatment, and community education presentation in schools and public meetings to stress the necessity for promoting animal welfare and limiting stray overpopulations. The Savannah Fund is an additional service, providing for the treatment and care of severely injured or ill stray animals.

To inform the general public about ARFP's services there are volunteers to help with the annual Book Fair, as well as Adoption Fairs. Each March, volunteers and foster animals participate in the Human Race, a 5K walk/run event to raise money for the organization. In addition, a yard sale takes place each spring to sell items gathered during the year by volunteers.

As of December, 2012, ARFP's Next Step Adoption Center has a new location, 711 Milner Drive in Greensboro, North Carolina, two doors from the former site. The new home provides greater space to house more homeless animals. It is open on Wednesday, Saturdays and Sundays. Call 336-574-9600 for operating hours.

Three days a week foster parents bring their foster pets to the adoption center for the public to meet. They also host a number of special events such as the Summer Open House and the Next Step Adoption Center Anniversary Celebration.

The NSAC has been welcomed into the community with open arms since it opened. Many generous volunteers and donors came to the rescue with a refrigerator, washer, dryer, and microwave, in addition to donating labor to help sand floors, lay tile, paint, and repair holes in ceilings. The Animal Rescue and Foster Program is proud of the next step it has made to help more homeless animals in the community. They have come a long way since 1992 and intend on taking even bigger steps for their next step.

Johnny - gato ordinario

Contributed by **Jean Cameron Tudor**, Edgewood, Washington

Johnny was a striped alley cat with brown-black fur. He came into our lives long ago, under unusual circumstances. It was 1976 in Hampton, Virginia during a very cold snap, with temperatures around eighteen degrees. One night we heard a kitten crying, but we couldn't locate it. The next night we heard the same cries and I went outside to see if I might find the source.

Finally, I saw a very tiny kitten running along the front of houses across the street and then around to the nearby waterfront. I tried to coax it to come to me, but it was very frightened and stayed away far enough that I couldn't catch it.

I figured it was living under one of the houses after possibly being dumped out on the street, so I talked to the woman living there, who gave permission for me to leave food out. But after a few days she stopped me from doing so, as she was hoping that the kitten would leave.

When the kitten grew hungry, it began to cry piteously. The lady gave in and let me feed it again. A day or two later I was able to get the kitten from under the house, but it bit and scratched wildly, causing me to let go. Our children announced that they would "get the cat." I suggested they wear gloves and take along something to carry it home in

That afternoon, they came in the door, funny looks on their faces, holding a brown paper bag containing a one-cat fight. They asked what they should do next. I suggested that they put the bag in the middle of the living room floor. Chaos ensued as that little kitten beat its way out of the bag, ran around the living room, climbed the drapes, ran up and down stairs, and ended up under our bed. We had to lift the mattress and the slats in order to get the kitten out.

The next day was a snow day from school, so we were all home. It would have been a quiet day had the kitten not been still wild. Eventually, however, it settled down some, and by late afternoon, when I held my hand down beside my chair, the kitten came over and sniffed it. Over the next few days we gradually became "sort of" friends.

We named the kitten Johnny. As he became accustomed to us and grew calmer, he turned into a very loving cat. Even though he never liked being held, he would curl up tightly against my leg. He liked to be able to touch people—but only on his own terms.

We made several moves after that, with Johnny along. In 1978, we left for Grosse Pointe, Michigan, that time with two cats, as we had added another one. The harsh winter in Virginia must have acclimatized Johnny, because he survived the cold Michigan weather for five years.

But then we prepared to leave for Indianapolis, and that brought on another Johnny "experience." Seeing the house packed with boxes and emptied of familiar furniture frightened him and we couldn't catch him when it came time for us to leave. The vet said to bring him in and they would give him a sedative. We did that and put it in a hamburger for him. I sat in the basement on the floor all morning until he wandered out and ate the hamburger. Once he was calm, we headed for Indianapolis.

Johnny lived with us there from 1983 to 1994. We think he was about eighteen when his health finally failed. Because I was leaving to teach in Venezuela, I wanted to leave him at the vet's where he would be cared for. The vet told me, however, that he didn't think Johnny would survive the week, so I had to face the idea of having him euthanized instead. It was a terrible decision to make, but I knew I'd rather be with him in his last moments than have him die broken-hearted without us. I petted him and loved him. The vet gave him a shot, and I petted him some more, loving him and crying as the light went out of his eyes.

Aura and Mr. & Mrs. B

Contributed by **Sue Henley**, Glendale, Arizona

Although Aura isn't a rescued horse, I share this story because he was a surprise package. When I bought his mother at an auction, I had no idea she was pregnant. I discovered him soon after we brought her home, in the corral, a newborn, and that was Aura, better known as BooBoo.

I learned that his father was a large quarter horse, his mother a little larger than a pony, which was an unusual pairing. I have come to treasure mother and son, who have formed an unexpected and beautiful addition to my life.

As for the "B" couple, they are bunnies.

An attorney I work for has his office at home. I called one day to say I had found a domestic bunny in a flower garden. Most of the bunnies around there are wild rabbits, but this one was definitely a domestic breed.

The attorney came over and helped me chase the elusive creature. He was able to catch it finally, and took it home.

We put up a sign in hopes that the owner would claim it, but instead we heard from another neighbor that she had found *another* one.

After a two-hour chase, the bunny was caught, and now there were two.

I learned of a vet who spays/neuters bunnies, so off they went for surgery. The attorney then built a fine hutch for them at my house, and I named them Mr. and Mrs. B. On good weather days they spend a few hours outside in a section of my yard that is safe for them. I do have to watch them, though, because they love to dig and dig!

We figure that someone bought them for Easter and tired of them after a while so turned them loose to live with the wild rabbits. But they live the good life now, in safety and comfort.

Jean Lafitte, Pierre, Bijou

Contributed by **Wendy Joseph**, author of *The Witch's Hand*, Wilmington, California

A guy came aboard the bus with a small carrier. Inside was a tiny tuxedo kitten staring back at me, very frightened. What got me were the white whiskers on her black face, unusual, I thought, as black fur generally produces black whiskers. Conversationally, I said, "Nice kitty. Are you taking her to the vet?"

"No, he said, "I'm taking her to the Pound."

I stared back at him. Animals at the City of Seattle shelter have seventy-two hours to be adopted before they're euthanized. "I'll take her," I said.

"Okay." He shrugged, accepting my offer.

So I got off the bus with a new kitty and a slew of issues. I was inclined to foster her until I could find someone to adopt her, but she was quickly taking hold of my pushover heart. I already had two cats. Would my landlord approve three? Would the other two, both neutered males, accept her? I thought docile Pierre would. His brother, Jean Lafitte, matched his namesake, however, a big piratical double Alpha male who entered a room by rearing up and thumping the door open, the gunslinger coming through the saloon doors.

I put the carrier down in the guest room. Pierre had gone into hiding. Jean Lafitte came in as I opened the carrier door. The poor little kitty had soiled herself, though she had not meowed much, and that in a scared, subdued manner. She looked at Lafitte. He looked at her. Then he hissed at her, long and loud. And that little girl pulled something out of

35

herself I never expected. She growled at him, not a trembling frightened kitten attempt, but a huge, long, big dog growl, menacing and mean. And Jean Lafitte? He ran into the closet in my room and stayed there the rest of the day.

Today the new kitty and tough Pierre curl up together and groom each other. And Bijou—what better name for a pirate's companion than a word meaning jewel?—found her meow, no doubt about it, and lets everyone know exactly what she's thinking—all the time.

Guilford County Animal Shelter

As is the case in many communities across the country, Guilford County Animal Shelter, located in Greensboro, North Carolina, is funded in part by the county and in part by private donations. When animals are brought to the shelter by animal control workers or private citizens, they go through an evaluation process to determine the state of their health and adoptability. While at the Shelter they receive medical care and nutrition, as well as other needed services such as grooming.

Volunteers and staff work with the rescues, teaching them how to relate to other animals as well as to those who care for them and to their future adoptive families. The Shelter publicizes stories of rescues, and provides a current listing of adoptable animals through their website. They also share their animal stories on Facebook and Twitter, and take animals to adoption gatherings in the area. The public is given information on how to be responsible pet owners when pets are taken to adoptive homes.

The story of Susie, included in this book, is one of their success stories that has been valuable in educating the public about the needs of strays, abused animals, and those from puppy mills, who so often end up in the Shelter. The Shelter receives animals from other areas when possible, where disasters such as floods and earthquakes have occurred leaving abandoned pets in their wake.

North Carolina made a significant contribution to penalizing animal abuse in 2010 through what is popularly referred to as "Susie's Law."

When Governor Bev Perdue signed the law, formally designated by the Senate as SB 254 and the House of Representatives as HS 1690, her action made history for animal care in the state. Both legislative bodies approved this measure despite opposition by those who would instead define animal abuse as a misdemeanor, rather than the Class H felony that the new law now dictates.

Prior to the enactment of the new law, anyone who would "maliciously torture, mutilate, maim, cruelly beat, disfigure, poison, or kill, or cause or procure to be tortured, mutilated, maimed, cruelly beaten, disfigured, poisoned, or killed, any animal" was guilty of a Class I felony, a lesser crime.

The law is named for Susie, whose story begins on August 2009. She was a puppy when she was set on fire and left to die. It was two weeks before she was found, lying in a local Greensboro park.

Although near death with second and third-degree burns on over sixty percent of her body, as well as suffering a broken jaw and teeth and covered with maggots, this small puppy had a will to survive.

The good news is that the puppy, now named "Susie," recovered, thanks to the care provided by the Guilford County Animal Shelter and its volunteers.

Susie quickly became a public celebrity. Her initial suffering triggered enough outrage in the community that county residents attempted to atone for the torment she went through by demanding better and more humane laws. The result was Susie's Law.

Susie attends fund raising events throughout the area. She even visited the North Carolina Legislature during the time the proposed law was on the agenda. She met many of the legislators in both houses, and won their hearts.

Much work continues to be done, but Susie is the poster dog for humane treatment for all animals. She is now living a happy, full life with her adopted mommy, Donna Lawrence. Together, Donna and Susie are spreading a message of hope, faith and forgiveness.

Angelina

Contributed by **Margaret Underwood**, Greensboro, North Carolina

Sometime around 1964, a friend alerted me to the fact that there was a dog hanging around the Colonial Grocery Store on Cloverdale Avenue in Winston-Salem, North Carolina. The guys in the meat department had noticed her, too. She was pregnant and they were giving her meat scraps out back.

She was of medium size, with light brown fur, a Shepherd mix, most likely. Later, the men told my friend Ann that the dog had had her puppies so we searched all over, but couldn't find her right away.

Across the street from the store in a lot which had been mostly cleared there was an uprooted hollow tree. Ann went to it, in case the dog was in it with her pups, and found the puppies way back inside.

We went every day to leave food. Angelina—the name we gave the mother—would try to lead us away from the spot, circling off toward the nearby woods, avoiding us. We'd crawl up inside the tree to try to get a look at the puppies.

At first, it was hard to tell, but I thought there were seven or eight of them. Eventually, the babies became more mobile and more adventurous. They began venturing out, making Angelina anxious.

Ann left a basket of food at the mouth of the tree every night. Early one evening, Ann discovered Angelina in the basket with her puppies. Ann threw her arms around her, throwing caution to the wind in her excitement, not knowing if she would be bitten. When she called me from her house and said, "Guess what?" I could hear the puppies yipping in the background and knew what had happened.

The pups and their mom had found a loving home. Angelina demonstrated her appreciation for us with affectionate licks and much tail wagging.

41

Ann and I found homes for all the babies once they were old enough to leave their mother. We then shared Angelina for many years. She held a very special place in our hearts.

Ginger & Mugsy Baja

Contributed by **Yvonne Kratz**, Wilson, North Carolina

Our dogs Ginger and Mugsy Baja tell of two different rescue experiences. Ten years ago, we heard of someone who found a Golden Retriever puppy under a bridge and brought her home. Interested, we went to meet this little dog.

She bonded immediately with my husband and he with her. So that very evening Ginger came home with us. The next day we built a pen and house for her so that she could be inside or out safely. She is still beautiful, and stays inside with us as part of our family when she isn't enjoying her outdoors home. She is a gentle and loving soul to everyone she meets, and we have been so grateful to have her in our family.

Mugsy Baja is a puppy mill refugee. I had seen an advertisement for Shih Tzu puppies and went to the address listed. It seemed strange to me that she brought the puppy out to me and I did not see any of the other dogs. I am wiser now, however, and know that that is one of the signs of a puppy mill.

I fell in love with the little puppy she showed me that day, and I took him home. He became Mugsy Baja.

After taking him to our vet for a thorough checkup, I learned that he not only had worms but also a cataract in one eye. But the vet took care of everything and he came home to live with us. That was seven years ago.

Since then, Mugsy Baja has developed heart problems, but is being well cared for. He is such a sweet dog and is the apple of my eye. I hope he will continue to live a long time with us.

Abby & Tux

Contributed by **Greg Lampe**, Chatham, New Jersey

On day in 2007 one of the rescues I worked with got a call from a neighbor who lives next to a known puppy mill. The owners had tied an old dog up to the post and left her there. We ran to her aid.

There was a note that said "The bitch bred for 13 yrs every cycle, no good anymore."

The Rat Terrier was in really bad shape. Our vet gave her less than a month to live. I determined that if she only had a month, it was going to be a good month. I took her home. My step kids and I named her Abby and set about nursing her back to health.

Three months to the day from when we got her, she gave birth to four pups. Two did not make it.

She was a proud, wonderful mother to the other two pups. The big pup we called Chow Fun, which means "big fat wide noodle". The very tiny pup we called Little One, then Tux, because he looked like he was wearing a tuxedo. Tux was so small he could fit in the palm of my hand until he was a year old.

Abby lived for another year with Tux by her side. Tux grew to weigh eighteen pounds. We know that his mother was a pure-bred Rat Terrier. We do not know how many male dogs donated, but we suspect more than one, because he has three different kinds of hair/fur. The Mohawk on his head grows naturally.

Tux turned three years old in January. During the day he follows me everywhere. He sleeps at my feet as I work. At night he has to be touching me. He is my constant companion dog, my buddy.

Tux is also a poet.

45

Here is a poem he wrote when I was away:

Woof! Woof!

Every single day
every single night
Every single moon
every single sun
When there is a sound near the door
I jump with excitement
hoping it's you I hear coming home
When I wake
I run to your room to see if you are
there
When I want to play ball
I run through the house looking for you
to play
I am just a dog and I don't understand
why I cannot find you when I look
My nose is strong
but you have gone too far away
But the memories I have of you
are deep and strong and will never fade
I will keep listening and looking for you
and believe in my heart you're looking for me too!
Someday soon we will see each other again
and we will snuggle and play ball and I will be happy once again!

How I Got into Animal Rescue

I got involved with animal rescue when I saved my first dog in 2000. I knew I wanted a Lab and that I wanted to rescue one. By chance I found a breeder on Yahoo Classifieds that noted the owner was going to put the last Lab of a litter down because no one

46

bought her. I agreed to make the four-hour drive to go and take a look. Upon arrival, I learned that the Lab was six months old, underfed, not cared for—and clearly not loved, as she had lived outside all winter. She had a dog house that she would climb on and then slide down on her rear, so she had sores on her legs and behind. The breeder, and I call her that loosely because I can think of worse and more fitting names, said that the reason no one wanted the Lab was because she is extra large-boned and would likely weigh between eighty and a hundred pounds when she was full grown, while most females of the breed are about sixty-five pounds. I haggled the woman down to $100, took the dog and left. My vet said she had mange and other issues. Needless to say, I called the authorities and Lab rescue on the "breeder," and I understand that she was never again allowed to breed dogs.

As for the rescued Lab, she became a member of our family, and received her real name: Lady.

Red Dog Farm

Red Dog Farm gets its name from a golden retriever named Rodney, the "Red Dog" who lived his fifteen years there with his people, Garland and Gary Graham. Since then, the Grahams have turned their residence into a place where domestic pets and farm animals live while waiting for adoption. The couple began by fostering golden retrievers in 2000 because of their love for Rodney. Soon, other dogs, as well as cats, ended up with the Grahams, where they were fostered and later adopted. The number of rescues increased when a barn was built to include farm animals. Six years later, after caring for over fifty animals, the Grahams began the nonprofit organization called Red Dog Farm Animal Rescue Network. A 501(c)(3) public charity, Red Dog is dedicated to rehabilitation, fostering and adoption of a variety of animals. Foster families volunteer to care for the animals prior to adoption. Lauren Riehle serves as Executive Director, with headquarters at 5803 Bur Mil Club Road, Greensboro, North Carolina 27410.

By the end of 2011, Red Dog Farm had taken in a total of one thousand three hundred and nineteen rescues.

49

Jake

Contributed by **Patsy Beeker**, Concord, North Carolina

Patsy runs a rescue program for cats and dogs, Kitty City, which involves an education program for children to learn how to provide safety and responsible care for animals. A community resource center in Cabarrus County, North Carolina, the center works with a variety of rescue efforts.

"Do dogs cry?" I asked the vet. He laughed.

The reason I asked the vet what he thought was because I saw Jake cry. Jake was a beautiful four-year-old Doberman. I had rescued him that spring, from a woman who fancied herself a rescuer but who had many dogs living in squalor and filth.

I don't know how Jake got there. He was surrounded by mostly mixed mutt breeds, over sixty of them crammed together in small dirty pens, howling and fighting and snarling at each other. He looked like a gentleman wrongly accused and thrown into Central Prison, an educated banker who stole paper clips and now lived with thieves who couldn't understand why he was in that hell. The dirty food bowls held bread scraps and stale pastries from a thrift store, the ones that had anything in them at all, that is. The other dogs fought over the scraps, but Jake stood with his head down, docked tail clamped tight against his bony thighs, eyes staring vacantly ahead. He didn't look at me on the other side of the fence as I spoke to him.

Somehow I managed to persuade the woman to give me Jake. I couldn't save the others, but I talked her into letting this one life escape that concentration camp. You see, I thought this dignified old soul was just sick and worn out. From the looks of him, I'd never have guessed that he would live much longer. The plan was to take him out of there and have my vet end his suffering. I would bury him in my field.

51

I led Jake away with a little piece of twine around his neck. Once we were headed to the car, his muzzle came up as he sensed freedom. He leaped into the back seat, almost sitting on top of me as my fellow rescuers drove us home. The stench of his skin infections was horrible. I lowered the window to breathe. Jake had already lost about thirty percent of his hair, and staph infections and starvation caused hair dander to rain down on my lap during the twenty-minute drive home. He looked at me every mile or so and tears rolled out of his eyes. I swear Jake knew somebody cared enough about him to save him.

This story ends well. The vet examined his teeth and pronounced him a young, healthy animal who would probably have starved to death without intervention. Antibiotics cleared up his infections, good diet repaired his glossy coat and put meat on his protruding bones, and loving care brought that elegant head and tail up in the air. The gleam came back to his eyes. After a month Jake found the perfect family who adopted him and showed him that all humans are not cruel and careless with their animals.

But I'll never forget that first day, in the peace and quiet of his new kennel at my house, with a clean bowl of water and real dog food in his own bowl, when Jake looked up at squirrels in the trees overhead and felt the clean breeze blowing across his bony spine. He looked at me and cried silent tears of joy. That night I heard Jake howl softly for just a moment before he went to sleep. It sounded strange, both mournful and triumphant, a sound I never heard him repeat.

Whenever we read stories about puppy mills and rescued dogs and cats and folks who face legal action in the courts because they neglect or abuse animals, it's impossible to see those pitiful furry faces and not feel outrage. Too often we forget after a few days what suffering the animals have endured, the emotional pain as well as the physical discomforts. But I can't forget. I saw Jake tell me in the most poignant way that he had felt pain and he was grateful that somebody took him out of there.

Do dogs cry? I know I do.

Adjustments

it's the learning that's so hard
learning that a hand coming toward you
will rub your ears and scratch your back
while you brace for the blows that don't come
nor yells that deafen, instead the soft murmur
from a face soft with sweet smell

Huge & Mabel: A Tudor Romance

Contributed by **Marina Julia Neary**, author of *Brendan Malone: The Last Fenian* and *Martyrs and Traitors*, Stamford, Connecticut

I have always been partial to adopting older animals. When my husband and I got married, we were twenty-one and thirty-one, respectively, both working crazy hours and trying to make most of the flourishing economy under President Clinton, in hopes of building a financial fund for the future baby.

After a long discussion, we realized that the most we could handle in the case of offspring would be a guinea pig. We went to a local family-run pet shop to look at some babies, but it was not the babies that caught our attention. In the corner we saw a giant black two-year old boar—the designation for male guinea pigs— perfectly healthy, free to a good home. The original owner had lost interest in keeping him and put the pet up for adoption.

To us it was a no-brainer. We brought him home the same night and did everything to ensure his comfort. He turned out to be extremely active and affectionate, grunting and squeaking in delight.

Among guinea pig breeders, it's customary to name their pets after various Shakespearean characters. Having published novels on the Irish Rebellion, a period of history that fascinates me, I named the new guinea pig Hugh, after Hugh O'Neill, Ulster's legendary chieftain, the Earl of Tyrone, who defied Queen Elizabeth.

Naturally, every Earl needs his countess, so we started looking for a suitable bride for Hugh. The trick was to find a female who had already given birth by the age of six months. If a female has not been bred by then, it's better not to breed her at all, as her hip joints become stiff, and it may be hard for her to give birth.

Hugh's bride was also a rescue pet. We saw her at another pet store where she was kept with her two grown children. Apparently, their claws were never clipped, so they continued rough-housing with their mom, leaving scratches on her belly. When we picked her up, her underside was covered in scabs. The store manager sold her to us for ten dollars.

We took her home, gave her time to heal and then placed her in the male's cage. His reaction was immediate and intense. He started purring, vibrating, huffing and puffing at the sight of a beautiful female of childbearing age. He spent the whole night chasing her around the cage. In the morning we found them snuggled contently under the log.

We named Hugh's mate Mabel, after Mabel Bagenal, O'Neill's hapless child-bride, Wife Number 3. According to Sean O'Faolain, O'Neill's biographer, "Women married early, and men married early and often." So we had a great Tudor-era romance under our roof.

Just a few weeks after bringing Mabel home, we noticed that she started expanding horizontally. Soon we were able to feel little kicks and twitches through the thin walls of her stomach. I used to flip her on her back and rub my nose against her warm belly filled with babies.

Guinea pigs are born fully formed and fairly independent, like miniature adults. They are not pink, blind and helpless. Far from it. They eat solid food and run around.

When we came to check on Mabel in the morning, we found her surrounded by her newly-born children scurrying all over her. She looked tired, and Hugh looked mildly annoyed, as he was not used to little ones crawling over his back and sniffing him.

The thing about guinea pigs is that the females ovulate an hour within giving birth. So by the time we removed the father from the cage, Mabel was pregnant again. Apparently, they had mated in that brief segment of time. Before we knew it, Mabel was expanding again. We had no trouble placing the little ones. She had four in the first litter with Hugh. Two went to a pet store, the same one that let us adopt Hugh, and the other two were placed with a family.

Mabel's subsequent litter was huge. Out of six babies, one died. Still, five surviving pups is an impressive litter. This time we gave them away to various Catholic schools in Pennsylvania as classroom pets. Two of them went to stay with one of the students for the summer, and the girl fell in love with them so deeply that she refused to return them at the end of the summer. They stayed with her as house pets.

In the summer of 2001 we decided that Mabel deserved to retire. I had a friend in Philadelphia who was looking for a pet, so I decided that Mabel would be perfect for her. Before handing Mabel over, I kissed her tummy one last time and asked her to wish me luck in getting pregnant. I was already twenty-two, with a steady job and enough in my savings account to support a baby, and to me Mabel represented motherhood and fertility. A few months later I was pregnant!

That was not the end of Mabel's work as a fertility lucky charm. She has helped two other women get pregnant. Both had struggled with infertility, but after coming in contact with Mabel, after stroking her fuzzy sides and her belly that had produced so many babies, they ended up having babies of their own. The gentle piggy was humorously canonized as St. Mother Mabel.

She died peacefully of old age on Easter in 2006. There is only one place she can be, and that's on the lap of St. Francis in heaven. Her legacy of gentle love and maternal joy continues on.

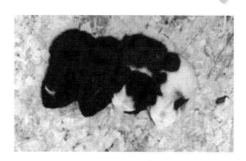

Roddy, Nikki, Peepy, Bruce, & Snarly

Contributed by **Dorothy Orgill Kirsch**, Memphis, Tennessee

I have had so many rescued pets that it's hard to count them all, but my five present companions each have a story to tell. Roddy, a mix of Jack Russell, Fox, and Rat Terrier, was hit by a car and ended up at my vet's. The owner wasn't to be located, but I was willing to visit him. My first time meeting him, he tried to bite me. Even so, he came home with me and has since has become a warm and loving dog, although quite protective. I'm not sure of his age, but he is an active presence in my life.

My oldest rescue is Nikki. She is a black and white Terrier mix, found in a crate with the door open, set on the hot sidewalk. Someone took her to The Humane Society where I met her. I just happened to be there when they brought her in. She has developed a sense of authority and has the idea that she is the head dog. I think perhaps that is so.

Another dog, Peepy—originally named PC for Patsy Cline—has now been named for a character in the novel *Bleak House*. A brown short-haired dog, she is a Katrina rescue and is very subservient, perhaps as a result of being in a small crate for a long time. Unfortunately, the other dogs tend to gang up on her, and I have to make sure she is protected.

Bruce, white Pomeranian and possible Cocker Spaniel mix, is still young. I have noticed that he is a very smart dog, but also at times a very destructive dog. He loves to chew up pencils, pens, books, paper, and anything else that attracts him. I hope that he will eventually outgrow that trait. He ended up with me after

59

being found wandering around in a high traffic area.

My newest is Snarly. She is a black and white Chihuahua, nine years old and rescued from a puppy mill. At first when I brought her home she was terrified of everything. She has overcome those fears and now is full of self-confidence. Her name at first was Carly, but because of her underbite, which makes her appear to be snarling, I changed her name to Snarly.

Eppi

Contributed by **Lois Slove Losyk**, Greensboro, North Carolina

She ran wild.
Wind in her hair, her brother
at her side, only freedom
on her mind. They wove in
and out of rush hour traffic
until someone scooped
them up.

The ad read:
"Two Britney Spaniels
Free To Good Home."
The rescuers introduced
us. Which one to choose?
Eppi gave us begging
looks, lapping licks, and
high flying jumps.
There was no choice.

She let us keep her
most times, unless the
wanderlust became too
great. Then she'd sneak
out an open door and bolt
for glorious new smells,
with an itch to see
exotic, faraway places.
Never a thought about
finding her way back.
Always, she would
make us get in the car
and search for her.

Left alone for
even an hour Eppi would
destroy a pillow or knock
over a lamp to let us
know she could leave but we
couldn't. She'd hide in a closet
and make us find her.

The last time she left
wasn't her choice.
It wasn't ours either.
It was her time and we
knew it.

When she couldn't walk
we lifted Eppi into the car,
rolled down the window,
and let the wind run wild
in her hair, to taste sweet
freedom one last time.

What About Overpopulation?

There is no doubt that the number of homeless dogs and cats outnumber pets who live with their human caregivers. The animal birth rate far exceeds that for humans. Statistics show that ten thousand humans are born in the U.S. daily, but according to estimates by the ASPCA®, some seventy thousand puppies and kittens are born each day. One consequence of these contrasting rates is that there will never be enough homes for all animals in this country. There are an estimated seventy million stray cats, but estimates are not as clear about how many stray dogs there are. Most of these strays, unfortunately, have not been neutered and, for the most part, live miserable lives, unwanted, often abused, ill fed, and with many health problems. We cannot ignore the importance of correcting such situations. The need to spay and neuter strays is obvious. The problem, of course, has to do with the costs of the programs and the rapidly increasing numbers of animals without homes. Of course there is also the huge cost to the taxpayers, estimated at two billion dollars a year, to find, shelter, euthanize, and dispose of "surplus" animals.

In the case of dogs, one unspayed female and her offspring have the potential to produce some 67,000 dogs over a period of six years. Yet fewer than three percent of dog owners take responsibility for these unplanned births. The expense of spaying female dogs is far less than that of caring for their litters. Add to that number the cat population. Both dogs and cat can reproduce up to two litters a year, with five—or more—puppies or kittens per litter. Approximately one animal per litter remains in its original home. The others end up abandoned or in shelters.

Statistics such as these make a clear case for the need for laws enforcing proper care of all animals, as well as the humane treatment of animals both domestic and wild. Communities must be prepared to provide adequate shelters for those in need of rescue and extended care. And while some states have better laws than others, it is necessary for uniform legislation throughout our country that will prevent puppy mills, animal hoarders, and other

63

situations contributing to the abuse of pets. Farm animals and large wildlife also need to have legislative protection from mistreatment and cruel forms of hunting.

We share this planet with all forms of life, and all life is in need and deserving of comprehensive, wise, and humane treatment. In cases when it is not feasible to avoid the death of any animal, or where euthanasia is recommended by veterinarians, laws are necessary requiring proper methods for ending life. We human beings are caretakers of this planet, and are called to be good stewards of those who been put in our charge.

Isabo, Maji, Maximum, Peppers, Widget, & Others

Contributed by **Sue Henley**, Glendale, Arizona

Our house has been home to many, many cats. There were several feral cats who hung out in the barn where our horse was boarded. Sad to say, many of their litters were taken by coyotes, but we managed to rescue three barn kitties, Isabo, Maximus and Maji. Isabo's sister was Max's mother, so they were cousins. Maji's mother was another stray.

Maximus had a very bad experience when he was about one year old: a car hit him and he suffered spinal cord injuries. My daughter, Somer, found him just after the accident and I had her call our vet to find a veterinary emergency clinic. We

were panicked, especially as we had gone through a series of pet losses over the year: Our seventeen-year-old horse, our sixteen-year-old dog, and our nineteen-year-old cat. We couldn't deal with another loss. The vet said to leave him overnight so that they could determine just how serious the injury to his spinal cord was. Not long after we left, however, she called to say the swelling in his vertebrae had increased. He could not feel her pinch his feet, nor could he move his tail. She recommended he be euthanized. My daughter and I insisted that she wait. "Just give him the night," I said. "He may just need some time."

Max made it through the night, and the next morning we took him to his own vet, who also could not give us much hope for his recovery. My prayers for his healing were continuous.

Later that day we went to see him, and we sensed that he wanted to go home with us. After careful instructions about his care, which included four weeks in a kennel, no exercise, antibiotics and pain meds, we took him home. Laying him on his blanket, we watched Max stretch and roll over, as if to say, "I'm going to be fine."

Three weeks later, Maximus gave me a present. At three a.m., he came out of his kennel, climbed up on my bed—with his front feet pulling him—and began purring and kissing me. I took that as his way of thanking me for not giving in to the vet's suggestion

In three more months Max was running through the house, jumping and running marathons with Maji and Isabo. He lived eight more years in spite of many visits to the vet for other problems.

He was a joy. He showed us love in return for ours. We were blessed by his presence all those years.

 Another cat, Widget, came to us under different circumstances. He was sitting on my neighbor's roof one rainy November night, about nine months old, lost, terribly thin. I placed a big bowl of food outside for him, but he would not let me touch him. The next night was a repeat. So I then fed him closer to our front door, keeping the screen closed. At that time he had not been neutered, and our rule is that only neutered pets are allowed indoors.

As Widget grew to know everyone in the house, he came in, had surgery soon thereafter, and is about seven years old now.

Two cats joined us along with my late husband: Slinky, a large black long-haired Persian, and Black Cat, although I call her Black Kitten. That one remains thin no matter how much food I put out for her, as she's a finicky eater.

As for our other cats, Maji is a polydactyl, with two sets of paws on his front feet and six toes each on his back feet, but backwards, with the little toe on the inside. His good friend is Peppers, whom Maximus brought home one day. I don't know how old he is, but thanks to Max he has become well fed.

Under the Porch

The petite mews begin in chorus
from that patted down spot
in dirt so old the bugs have left.
We crawl under the porch to find
the source, shine a light
on the large gray-striped cat
who dares us to disturb her brood.
We back out, prepare a plate
of leftover tuna loaf,
place it near, but not too near,
leave quietly and wait.

When the time is right
she will come to us
parading the little ones
who follow blinking
into the brightness of this day.

Stella

Contributed by **Sherman Bamford**, Roanoke, Virginia

Stella was the friendliest, sweetest dog I have ever known. Some statistics about her include that she was a beagle/hound mix weighing about forty pounds. She was about a year old at adoption and lived to be eleven years old.

Stella was a gift from my sister, Martha. Martha gave me a "coupon" so that I could adopt a dog at the Roanoke, Virginia SPCA® animal shelter in the fall of 2000. At that time, the animal shelter had a glut of lost or abandoned animals and had a difficult time placing them in good homes. Unfortunately, this is still true today in the Roanoke Valley, even though there are more adoption agencies today than in 2000.

I went to the shelter several times before deciding to adopt Stella. The shelter offered a small pen where I could take a prospective pet and play with it before deciding whether we were a good match. When the attendant let Stella in the pen, she immediately ran towards me and into my arms. Some of the other dogs I had seen were friendly, but not to the same degree. Strangely enough, at that moment I thought I could see the love in her heart manifesting itself.

I adopted her immediately. I was not mistaken. Stella was a very social dog. She liked to be around people and she liked to be around other dogs. Whenever a dog or person came around, she would introduce herself, in dog-like fashion. I never saw her growl at another dog or person except in self defense, and only on rare occasions. I used to joke that if a burglar broke into my house, she would be more of a "greeter" than a guard dog. She was very close to me throughout her entire life and was great company.

When I first took her home, I let her out into the back yard and she would not stop howling. I was worried about this and other problems she had, and immediately signed her up for an obedience class. It turned out that the inappropriate behavior was only temporary nervousness on her part. She did well in the class, and I think the class helped both of us.

Stella became my most dependable hiking buddy. In the year after I adopted her, we moved to Kentucky and then Montana where I had jobs monitoring forests. Stella would join me for countless hikes for work or play—although she regarded them all as play, of course. In Kentucky, we hiked along the ridges above the Rockcastle River. In the Rockies, we hiked in the national forests around Missoula. One of the trips was a four-day backpacking trip in Idaho around the Mallard-Larkins roadless area and the Vanderbilt Hill area. As we were leaving the trailhead, we heard a horseman mention that there were wolves around. On one night of the trip we heard wolves howling to the left of us, several ridges away. On the next night, we heard wolves howling on the right of us, from a distance. Fortunately, the wolves didn't come close enough to bother us. We did move back to Virginia the next spring, and a friend who was watching Stella one weekend told me that she saw Stella running out of the woods with a coyote. So maybe Stella learned something from the wolves in Idaho.

In Virginia, my job again involved forest monitoring. As part of my job, I would bushwhack through the woods far from any trails—and Stella would come along. I would look for creeks or rare plants at the sites of proposed timber sales or illegal motorized vehicle trails while Stella kept her nose to the ground, seeking out new scents and adventure. Our bushwhacks ranged throughout western Virginia, from the High Knob and Pine Mountain areas south and north of the coalfields of far southwestern Virginia, to Mountain Lake near Blacksburg, to the Allegheny Highland area at the headwaters of the James River, to Big Schloss above the

Shenandoah Valley.

Stella always made sure she remained within earshot. She loved to tromp around in the woods, but was very wary of losing me. I'm sure she dreaded the uncertainty that would involve. The only exception was when her social nature began to take over and when other dogs were involved. On two or three occasions she caught the scent of numerous other dogs and sought them out, forgetting about me entirely. One time, I joined my sister on a hike in snowshoes at New World Gulch in Montana. Little did we know that the site was a popular winter hike for people and their dogs and that there were numerous loop trails throughout the area. Stella caught the scent of other dogs and followed the loop trails around and around until just before dark, while we waited impatiently at the trailhead, worrying that she would not come back.

Another time, after hiking up and down Warm Springs Mountain in Bath County, Virginia, Stella detected the smell of numerous dogs in front of her and followed them. They were hunting dogs being trained as part of the Labor Day bear hunting season. Stella was taken into the truck with the hunters and was taken to Bath County animal control. We called the office the next day and retrieved her. She looked happy and quite pleased with herself.

Last year, at the end of August, I took Stella in for a regular physical examination, and the veterinarian heard a muffled sound when she listened to the area around her heart with a stethoscope. X-rays indicated that the cause of the muffled sound was a lung tumor. She was expected to live for about a month and a half.

We gave her pain medicine, anti-inflammatory medicine, and medicine for vomiting and made sure she was comfortable and got plenty of rest for the next few months. We took her on one final trip, to the Eastern Shore of Virginia, keeping her in an air-conditioned motel as much as possible. Her last hike was a short walk to a beach next to the Chesapeake Bay, where a fresh breeze was blowing. She required a lot of rest at this time, but seemed to be very appreciative that she was given the opportunity to go on one last hike. She lived a month and a half longer, which was twice as long as her life expectancy at the time of the diagnosis.

During the last two days, she became unable to walk without collapsing. She was put to sleep on the Monday after Thanksgiving.

Throughout those last three months, she remained strong and her attitude remained positive. Dogs have "separation anxiety" when the people they love are gone; I felt the same kind of "separation anxiety" after Stella was gone and the house became quiet.

Stella's ashes were buried at a secret place beside one of our favorite hiking trails.

Postscript:

This March, we took in another dog, Jake. Jake is a blue-tick hound dog. He was found wandering around, hungry, in a Forest Service campground, many months after hunting season ended. He is defensive and still a little wild. Although attempts were made to find his owner, we heard nothing. Because of his "wild and woolly" nature, we are not sure how this story will end, but we know he has a good heart. Oh, and I have enrolled him in obedience school.

Lovey

Contributed by **Martha Shannon**, Greensboro, North Carolina

My life with Lovey began in December 2010, when I sent an email out to someone who was keeping a small dog for the Montgomery County Humane Society near Troy, North Carolina. "I'm thinking about a little dog. It would help me be more active and a better housekeeper. What do you think?" I had learned she was caring for a small Feist, who might be just the right pet for me.

The answer came, describing Honey. "She is a sweetheart. She's not crazy about cats. She doesn't hurt them, just runs them up a tree. We think she is about five or six years old. We found her in our lot one day when we came home, so maybe someone had passed away and the family dropped her here knowing we would care for her. But she doesn't know where she came from. She is great indoors and would make a wonderful house dog."

I traveled to meet Honey, and the minute I saw her I knew she needed to come home with me. I paid her fees and asked to have her spayed, after which I would pick her up. Someone else then fostered her until I was able to return for her. Her new foster caregiver emailed me: "She is such a sweetie. She loves her dog bed. The other day when she got back here after her surgery, she found the blanket I had thrown on her bed. It was folded up, but she proceeded to unfold it and spread it out on her bed with her mouth! She is a funny little dog when she raises her lips to greet you with a smile. She does not like the cold, so I know she will enjoy her coat. She also does not like to pose for the camera. Thank you for helping her. I prayed for a Christmas miracle with Honey and you answered!"

On Christmas Eve, a teacher from the school drove me back to Montgomery County Humane Society to pick her up. By then I had decided that "Honey" wasn't a name I particularly cared for, so I chose "Lovey," from Danny Kaye's Hans Christian Anderson song, "No Two People Have Ever Been So in Love."

When we returned to Greensboro she had a bath appointment at PetSmart to take care of her fleas and bad smell.

At home, she had to be lifted up the kitchen steps, because she was too fat to climb them.

A month or so later, her smile finally returned, so I guess she figured she really was home. We walk thirty to forty minutes twice a day, and she comes to work with me at the church Thursdays and Fridays, where I am Office Administrator. Everyone loves her. A three-year-old at our church school will sit with her for long stretches of time.

I gave her some rawhide bones but she hides them instead of eating them. Whenever I find them, she takes them from me and hides them again, wagging her tail. Her little tail wags almost all the time. She is a blessing and wonderful fun for me.

74

Cabarrus CARES & Kitty City

Cabarrus CARES—Coalition of Animal Rescue Efforts and Services—is an organization in Cabarrus County, North Carolina, formed in 2003. An advocate for animals, the Coalition cooperates with and assists other rescue organizations. Members serving on the Coalition are on various councils, advisory panels, and other boards for the purpose of promoting the well-being of pets.

Providing pet oxygen masks for first response fire vehicles was one of their early services. Volunteers help promote and educate the public about spay/neuter programs. Humane adoptions is only one of their goals. Educating the community on how to care well for pets already owned is another priority.

Its first project was to equip a Pet Food Pantry in Kannapolis, North Carolina when ten thousand residents lost jobs after a large textile corporation declared bankruptcy. The Pantry supplied food and supplies to families with pets for three years, during a time when family budgets could not afford those items.

In addition, other services were provided to the general public, such as free rabies vaccinations and low-cost spay/neuter programs.

An Indigent Care Account was set up for pet owners who encountered emergency situations with their animals. Members of CARES fed orphaned kittens and puppies and began a foster program leading to pet adoptions.

Unforeseen needs have been another focus for CARES, as in the case of puppy mill busts, or when rescue and disaster relief efforts are needed.

Educational opportunities take place in the area schools, church groups, 4-H Clubs, and scout troops, where youngsters are taught how to treat animals with compassion, and how to use proper care and handling of pets.

Kitty City is a CARES project for animal education, pet rescues, and adoptions. It is a non-profit organization and a no-kill shelter, one of the few in the state. Stories of a few of those animals are in this book, as told by the Director, Patsy Beeker

Amy & Sandy

Contributed by **Sue Henley**, Glendale, Arizona

We have had several dogs. Amy is a Golden Retriever-Yellow Lab mix who was not accustomed to being around other dogs. Her owner had died and I was planning to foster her. Our Tasha, whose best friend Buster had recently died, was overjoyed to meet Amy and so, instead, Amy joined our family. When Tasha died at age eighteen, Amy was nearly thirteen. We were glad to provide her a home for her later years. We were fortunate to have her.

About the same time Amy arrived, we welcomed Sandy, the puppy who came with my daughter's fiancé. Sandy's leg was broken, but it took two weeks for the fiancé to take her to the vet's for treatment, where he was advised that it was too late to set the leg, so she has a limp. She stayed on with us but the fiancé is gone. She is about the size of Amy, but we aren't sure of her breed.

Scooter is a small wire-haired dog who showed up in our yard while my late husband was watering the lawn. She would run up to him and then run away. While I was in the house getting a cookie to lure her back, she ran back across the street. We saw two women who had been driving by and were trying to catch her before she was hit by a car. But they were unsuccessful.

After that she ran up to some people walking their dogs, while my husband called out to me, "If you can grab her, I'll take her." But that didn't work, either.

So I put up a sign, but even though someone called who had seen her two weeks earlier in another neighborhood, no one claimed her.

My husband wrestled with his belief that we just couldn't take in another dog, but then would say, "I sure like that dog!" I figured that although we had two big dogs, she was little and we could add her to our pet family.

A few days later we went to ride our horses and, after some discussion, the die was cast. When we came home, he went outside, and a little while later came in to say, "Well, your dog is on her way home."

That meant our home, and now she runs the house.

Misty

Contributed by **Julie Shelburne**, Greensboro, North Carolina

Misty came to us from the Guilford County Animal Shelter when she was about a year and a half old. It was the first part of December 2008. Before we went to the shelter we looked through the available dogs pictured on their web site so we had some idea of what we'd find. When we got there, the place was so loud with the barking and jumping up of the dogs in their small kennels that we found it difficult to make a decision. The ones we had picked out on the web site didn't seem to be the "right" dog once we saw them. So we left, planning to return later.

The next time our daughter went with us. Somehow we let a dog out by accident, which brought a volunteer to help us, and that made all the difference. She showed us two dogs, and although we liked them both, we chose the slightly smaller one with short hair a pretty shade of brown. What convinced us was that she walked with us easily and also chased a ball playfully. She obviously loved the volunteer with us, who told us the dog, named Misty, had been there about six months. That was a surprise to us. We knew this would be our dog and signed the papers while Misty waited patiently. She also was well behaved in the car on the way to a pet store when we picked up some items for her before heading home.

The next day we took her to the vet. She determined that Misty was a "Dingo," sometimes called a "Carolina Dog." This breed is smaller than the Australian Dingo by about forty pounds. In researching the Carolina Dog, we learned that it is a pariah dog, from the general name in India for half-reclaimed dogs in villages with no particular owner. They are always ready to accompany someone on a hunting expedition. Another interesting fact is that it is one of the few existing breeds that is truly a "primitive dog," developed by natural selection for survival. Even today it is not a completely domesticated canine.

Some typical characteristics that we see in Misty are that her ears and tail are always up and she is gentle, social, and intelligent, neither aggressive nor destructive. Her speed and strength in running is amazing, which we noted right away in our large fenced-in yard and our mountain place. In fact, at the beginning we were unable to take her for a simple walk, even when she was harnessed. It took obedience classes for her to learn simply to walk along with us, and as a quick learner she was a good example for her classmates during that time. My husband Palmer and I are lucky to have her as our companion, and we are so proud of what she has achieved.

Beamer

Contributed by **Patsy Beeker**, Concord, North Carolina

I have a newspaper article on my desk that says animals have no souls, no spiritual values or connections, and they just exist at the mercy of humans. That's an interesting thought. It made the person who brought me the article very angry. My reply: who am I to determine such weighty issues as souls and theology when it concerns a lot of humans as well as the animals? She and I can safely agree, however, that anyone who believes that possession of an extra pair of legs keeps you from having a guardian angel has never spent much time in animal rescue!

The perfect example of that is a little black one-eyed cat named Beamer who currently lives at Kitty City in Concord. He won't be there long, I think, as he has some special kind of sweetness that makes all visitors reach in to stroke his scarred little head. It's almost as though rubbing Beamer gives you good luck, like rubbing the Buddha statue's belly. I don't know about that, but Beamer is most deserving of a few good head rubs.

Beamer was found on the side of the highway on a ninety-five degree day by a Department of Transportation worker who was picking up the body of the kitten's dead mother. The tiny kitten was injured, but alive. How many hardened sweaty guys picking up roadside debris have the heart to reach down and save a tiny black kitten who could barely mew because he was so thirsty? Clearly the guardian angel was working hard to send the perfect person Beamer's way.

After a few bites of a hot dog, Beamer traveled to the only rescue center where someone answered a phone call in the middle of the afternoon. As luck would have it, I was there to give the okay for him to come to Kitty City. His story was heartbreaking, but I didn't really have much hope for him. When I saw how badly damaged his eye was, I sent him straight to the best emergency vet I know with the expectation that Dr. Roberts would put him down mercifully. A head injury like that is no simple matter. But within the hour, Dr. Roberts called and said "I can fix that."

"Sure," I answered, "but can I afford that?" Not to worry; the office staff had already fallen for Beamer's story and started taking up a collection to pay for his surgery. The guardian angel was kicking into overtime. How could I deny this kitten the chance to survive?

So Beamer had the eye removed; his head scars are now growing fuzzy new hair, and he likely does not remember having vision on both sides of the head. Just as we can't see behind us, Beamer probably thinks that everyone sees only what lies to the left side. He's charmed everyone, and my folks walk around with him cradled like a little two-pound toy to see all the good things his life will offer him. I swear that kitten has the face of a cherub.

Throughout his recovery, I kept thinking of a lovely young woman who worked with Dr. Roberts and who had such passion for helpless babies like this. Laura Beam passed away last spring, but I suspect that from her perch in the heavens, she has a special watch out for the helpless and the needy. It's the sort of kitten Laura would have swept up and cuddled as she worked.

Several people tagged names on the little guy, but I had no doubt who he would be named for. I think his guardian angel just has to be Laura Beam. Who else would have sent the perfect DOT worker to bring this fellow to the right rescue and to guide him to her boss and her friends to touch everyone's heart?

So do you still believe there's no spiritual connection looking out for animals? If you read the Bible, you know the verse about "His eye is on the sparrow." Surely, Someone had an eye out for a plain little black kitten who needs that extra eye, any way he can get it. And surely, if Laura is looking out for these helpless creatures, heaven is a pretty happy place.

American Society for the Prevention of Cruelty to Animals®

The ASPCA® has a long history in this country. Founded in 1866 by Henry Bergh, and now one of the largest humane societies in the world, it was the first one to be established in North America. The ASPCA® headquarters is located in New York City. It is a 501(c)(3) corporation with over a million supporters across the United States, serving as the nation's leading voice for animal welfare. Its mission is to provide effective means for the prevention of cruelty to animals throughout the United States.

The Society works in three key areas: community outreach, animal health services, and anti-cruelty initiatives. They are active in many locations, working with shelters and rescue operations. The organization offers a wide range of programs, including a mobile clinic outreach initiative, its own humane law enforcement team, and a groundbreaking veterinary forensics team and mobile animal CSI unit.

In 2007, the ASPCA® entered into three-year partnerships with animal welfare and community organizations in specific "target communities" around the country to launch ASPCA® Partnership, dedicated to providing positive outcomes for animals at risk.

Scarlett, Kodie, and Mojo

Contributed by **Josette Swain**, Greensboro, North Carolina

Scarlett is my latest rescue. She had been living with some people who could no longer take care of her. I wanted to give her a good home, so I agreed for her to live with me. She is a six-month old Doberman with a loving attitude toward everyone she meets. She is high energy and a very quick learner. My rescue Mojo, however, who enjoys quiet time, wonders what I did to ruin his serenity.

Two of my other rescues are Mojo, as I referred to, and Kodie. Kodie was my golden girl. I rescued her from a neglected situation when she was two. I knew she had to come home with me when I saw the ex-husband of the woman I got Kodie from kick her in the face when she jumped up to greet him. The woman gave her to me immediately. Kodie was the sweetest girl ever! I lost her in April, 2011 and still miss her so much, but I am glad to know I gave her a loving home for her last years.

Mojo is a Bassett-Bloodhound mix that I rescued about five years ago. His owner had to go into a nursing home and her children put all three of her dogs into the shelter. Mojo was not only separated from his owner but from his siblings. I saw him at an adoption fair and noticed that he was not receiving any attention, probably because he was not a puppy or the cutest one there. I felt so sorry for him that I had to take him home. Mojo understands that he has been rescued and shows appreciation for the attention he now receives. He is a very sweet dog—even though he peed on my statue of St. Francis!

Deacon

Contributed by **Marion Seaman**, Greensboro, North Carolina

Our Sheltie had been dead for over a year when our daughter insisted that it was time to get another dog to be a companion for our flat-coated retriever. One Saturday afternoon we went to the animal shelter, a trip that I truly dreaded as I knew I would want every single dog in every single cage and go home despairing over the conditions that they endured each day until adoption, or worse.

I unwillingly accompanied my daughter into the shelter, telling her with each step we took that I wasn't ready for a new dog. I was really telling myself that I couldn't stand the thought of looking at all of these homeless dogs and knowing that I couldn't help them. We walked up and down the rows and I had a reason for not touching each dog: he's too big, he's too small, I don't want another black dog, he doesn't look friendly, and so on. I had managed to get through the first room and we were halfway through the second and last room when all of my reasons ran out. In the cage before us were two dogs. One ran up to the door and barked, but the other lay on the cold concrete floor and looked up at us with incredibly appealing eyes. I suggested we try that one, since he didn't seem as excitable as all of the others.

The Beagle that we took out in the play yard was thin and very quiet. He liked being petted, but was very lethargic. When he sniffed our current dog, they seemed to get along, so we paid the money to adopt him. He had to be neutered and we could pick him up on Friday.

When we went to get him, our new Beagle was still under the effects of anesthesia and very docile. He sat in the back seat with our daughter as we drove home and debated his new name. Since he had typical Beagle coloring—black with caramel and white—we decided he was close enough to the black and gold of Wake Forest University to be their mascot. He immediately became Demon Deacon.

We decided to call him Deacon, ultimately a great cosmic joke. We took Deacon to our vet on Saturday to find out that one reason he was so lethargic was because of a terrible mouth and sinus infection from bad teeth. He needed to have sixteen teeth removed and start on antibiotics right then. Deacon went back to the vet on Monday for his extractions and came home, once again under the effects of anesthesia.

Once Deacon shook off the effects of his surgery, he decided to live up to the "Demon" portion of his name. Not letting the lack of a full set of teeth bother him, Deacon decided to eat plastic CD jewel cases, the squeakers from all dog toys, the filling from his dog bed, the plastic mask from a sleep apnea machine, and a pound and a half of chocolate candy. He eats hard kibble rather than soft dog food, loves to chew on rawhide sticks, and loves to police our yard and eat all available acorns. His tongue lolls out of his mouth in the summer, since he lost one of his lower canine teeth.

Rather than having rescued a calm and docile Beagle, we find ourselves completely amused— and bemused—by a loving Beagle that just wants to live life to the fullest and have a great time.

Postscript: After this story was written, Deacon became seriously ill. His diagnosis was advanced canine lymphoma, and we had to euthanize him. We miss him, but hope that by finding a place in this book he can continue to live on in a small way.

Quincy

Contributed by **The Reverend John Hartman**, Greensboro, North Carolina

Our beloved dog, Quincy, born in August 1997, and most likely a poodle/bishon mix, entered our lives during Christmas 2005. Our family had not owned a dog up to that time, but through Heaven and Earth Animal Rescue Team— HEART— from Franklinton, North Carolina, we responded to a request to foster Quincy over the holidays, just to try it out with our children, who had been putting the full court press on to get a dog. Talk about a sucker's play. Did anyone really believe that I was going to be able to give Quincy back after Christmas vacation was over? I knew in my heart that he was here to stay. Here we are over six years later, with Quincy very much a family dog, and we do not regret our decision one bit.

Quincy came to us with a multitude of physical issues. First, he was malnourished, and most likely neglected; his left ear was partially mangled in a dog fight and required several stitches. During the visit to the veterinarian, a tumor was discovered near Quincy's backside. It was biopsied, and then the bad news came: cancer. Surgery was quickly scheduled, and successfully completed. However, it was noted that while the tumor was localized to that one area near his hind quarters, it was unfortunately the type of cancer that normally spreads. Still, like Old Man River, Quincy just keeps rolling along. He has never had any more issues with tumors or cancer, and he has brought us much joy into our lives and home as a loving, caring, pet.

Some Cats, Some Dogs (and their friends)

Contributed by **Patsy Beeker**, Concord, North Carolina

I found this prayer to help me during the difficult days with our rescued animals needing so much help, knowing we can never make life for them as good as it should be. It is attributed to Albert Schweitzer, but I don't know who the actual poet is:

Hear our humble prayer, O God,
for our friends the animals,
especially for animals who are suffering;
for animals that are overworked,
underfed and cruelly treated;
for all wistful creatures in captivity
that beat their wings against bars;
for any that are hunted or lost or deserted
or frightened or hungry;
for all that must be put death.
We entreat for them all Thy mercy and pity,
and for those who deal with them
we ask a heart of compassion
and gentle hands and kindly words.
Make us, ourselves, to be true friends to animals,
and so to share the blessings of the merciful.

After rescuing over three dozen cats from a hoarder who had kept over a hundred captive in his house, I went in this afternoon to work with our newest residents at Kitty City. There is comfort in familiarity in the worst of times, and the routines of their horror were less frightening to them than our deliverance had been. I was disgusted yesterday at the filth, at flea dermatitis and swollen wormy bellies as we lifted the cats from their carriers. They were in no mood to be treated then. Today, after giving them a little time to settle down, it was time to inventory.

I don't think I saw the nearly hairless little Siamese mix

yesterday who was gently squared away in her cage. Her hair really is no color at all, just sort of blending in with her gray skin that is mottled with pink rashes and scabs. A corneal ulcer scars her left eye. She struggles against swallowing a Capstar to kill fleas and a mouthful of Strongid to begin attacking all sorts of worms in her body. Tonight may be the first time in her life that she sleeps without twitching and scratching herself raw. She doesn't understand that I want to hold her tight against me and cry for her, or that maybe next week she'll start being beautiful to everyone else when her hair grows back fuzzy and golden. She wants only to squirm away to the back of her cage.

The pregnant white cat is different. She wants to be held, and I can't because of her awful wounds. I can only scratch her head and promise her it will be better soon. Some cats stare defiantly, some glare at me, and some shrink behind litter boxes in hope that I don't see them at all.

I spend a moment with each one to reassure them. My helper, Jimmie, and I move down the line attacking fleas and worms and soothing them.

The Siamese had one of the worst conditions. Some of the others look almost normal, with flea scabs that I find only when I rub their heads or spines. But a few others are in dismal shape. I can't even talk about it. I know that the vet will end their suffering tomorrow, as the poem says, with *"a heart of compassion and gentle hands and kindly words."* It's the least we can do for them, and also the best, to end their misery away from the hellish place where they endured their lives.

I've seen the suffering before, and I know I'll see it again. Animals are amazingly resilient. Mentally, maybe they are stronger than humans. It is a blessing that they don't have logic, can't read, don't know that humans shouldn't let them get this way. Do they understand when we release them?

About eight years ago I had the privilege of working with wonderful folks who helped me staff a food ministry for pets of unemployed humans. I will never forget the Saturday when a man brought in a dog who was so sick that the best thing I could do was pay the vet for the injection to end her pain. He didn't intend to let it get that bad, but he had no money to stop the infection before she reached crisis status. He really loved that dog. He knew by my face that his dog was dying. He was embarrassed at the tears running down his face. "I guess you get used to stuff like this," he said sadly, as though I was some kind of super authority who shrugged off death every day. "I reckon I ought not to cry. I bet you don't cry any more, you've seen a lot of this."

I was fighting tears for him as well as for the dog whose eyes told me she knew she was dying. I can't ever forget the look she gave me when I rubbed her feverish head. "No," I said, "I do cry. I just try to hold it back and not cry in front of people. I hope I never get to the point that I don't cry."

So tonight, as I drove home alone and listened on my radio to an organ recital of one of my favorite hymns, I just pulled over and had a good bawl for all the suffering and for the folks who will hold a little fur-covered head and speak softly until it is all over. As the old hymn puts it:

"And when in death I'm free, I'll sing on, I'll sing on.
And when from death I'm free, I'll sing and joyful be,
And through eternity I'll sing on."

I had a vision in my head from yesterday, with all those cats racing in terror from us in that stinking house because they didn't understand we were there to save them. My assistant, Dave, and I entered a room where a parrot sat silently in a big dirty rusted cage in the middle of the floor, with about a dozen cats lounging around him. I thought of what it must be like to be a bird surrounded by cats, the natural enemy of birds, and to know that my normal lifespan was six decades beyond the best any of those cats would endure. We could hardly breathe in the acrid fumes inside that house, and I know birds are very sensitive to bad air. But the bird was doomed to stay there and live on.

"And when in death I'm free, I'll sing on." Is that when the parrot will break his silence?

I had a good cry for that bird and for those cats and for dogs I will never see again except in my head—dogs who suffered and frequently died, sometimes because they were lucky.

I am so grateful for folks like Jimmie, who give up a whole Sunday afternoon to clean dirty cages and will struggle against broken teeth and sharp nails to shove a Capstar pill down an unwilling throat, shirt stained with slime and spit-out medicine and his fingernails with a good bit of his own blood caked around them.

I am so grateful to know men like Andrew, who will stay with a dying cat until well past midnight because he knows *panleuk* will steal the life soon and he does not want to let her die alone. I am grateful for women like Denise, who sleep beside tiny kittens and wake to nurture them hourly as they fight for life, and in spite of losing the fight, she will do it again next time because so few people *can* do it.

I am honored to know people like Sharon, who will make the last day of a dying dog's life the best ever, surrounded by love and good thoughts and clean bedding. People like Marlene and Ruby and Sherry who go out by moonlight and streetlight to feed homeless animals in rain and snow and summer heat. People like Betsy Carpenter who go against the grain because humans won't do right by their animals. I am humbled by the dozens of friends who spend their time every week, some every day, to clean and feed and try to find good homes for animals.

I am so blessed with so many friends who have the hearts of compassion and the gentle hands and kind words. This is my prayer of thanksgiving.

Cages

wire, steel, boards, mark bounds
of detention or safety, or breeding,
lack the one defining feature
required: freedom to leave
their squalid enclosures—
yet those enslaved by fortune
hunters make do, endure
the only life they know,
unaware of hope, with space shared
only for mating, they bring forth
more who will be caged
until sold or left to die
and thus pay the price
captured by others' greed

Victoria

Contributed by **Sandra Barnes**, Greensboro, North Carolina

When I was in my twenties, single, living and working in San Francisco, I came across my first rescue. That was the day a scraggly, coughing puppy stumbled down the sidewalk in front of the advertising agency where I worked, so I went out and picked her up. She was shivering, poor little thing, obviously quite unwell. I took her to a local veterinary hospital, and we ran a notice on the radio station "Pet Patrol" with her description, hoping her owner would come and get her.

No one responded. The vet was not encouraging. He said she had mange, but he could not do anything about that immediately because she also had Parvo and she was probably going to die. She had touched my heart, and I asked him to do what he could for her. I didn't name her because she was so sick and would surely die.

I lived in an apartment that did not allow pets, so I smuggled her in and out under my coat or in a shopping bag. Every day at lunch I had to rush home and get her, take her to the hospital for a shot, and then smuggle her back home. She was so weak she couldn't stand or sit; I had to hand-feed her, and hold her up when she had to potty. The mange took over with a vengeance. Her hair fell out, her skin turned black and wrinkled, she was sick and pathetic and ... well, she was going to die.

Several weeks into this adventure I came home from work, popped a record on the record player, and started mixing up the formula I had to feed this puppy. I was listening to an operatic soprano, Victoria de los Angeles, and going about my business as usual. When the soprano hit a very sustained high note this sickly little puppy struggled to her feet, threw her head back, and howled. That was the turning point—and of course I had to name her Victoria.

Victoria was making great progress when I informed the vet I was moving to Denver. He told me to find a vet before I found a job or a place to live. He gave me all the records, warned me that she had to keep on with her medicines for a while longer, and said that she would probably never have hair again.

In Denver I quickly found a vet and turned over Victoria and her records so he could continue with her treatment. He told me there was an experimental drug being used for mange and he'd treat her for free if I would allow him to try it on her. He did not know if it would help, but was certain it would not hurt. So we did it.

Within a week, Victoria had a peach fuzz of hair all over, even her totally bald head and tail. Within six months, Victoria became a beautiful, fully coated little dog, healthy and happy and devoted. She eventually moved across the country to Greensboro with me, met and married Ralph with me, and settled into a happy long life.

Victoria was with me for sixteen years.

Apache

Contributed by **Stephanie McManus**, Greensboro, North Carolina

I have a miracle named Apache. He's a yellow Lab mix we got at the Humane Society back in 2008 when I learned my father only had a few months to live due to esophageal cancer. This dog has brought me endless joy.

When I first met Apache, then called "Dusty", he was sitting alone in a crate curled up with his eyes open, staring at the middle of the room. He didn't make any noise, but every other dog in the small room was barking loudly. I went up to him and asked the employee at the Humane Society if he was sedated for some reason. She said, "No, he just sits there like that." I looked at him more closely and his tail wagged a little. I noticed one of his eyes was drooping and leaking a bit. He seemed uncomfortable. I was already reaching out to him. The staff said he had been found wandering alone, abandoned by his mother or owner. He was about four months old.

They let us take Dusty home for a trial run. He was really confused at first, and we struggled with teaching him not to pee in the house. It honestly drove me a little crazy. We purchased Dusty his first toy, which was a yellow duck that squeaked, and he loved it.

During this time, I was in Florida, driving from Gainesville to Kissimmee, back and forth to be with my father and care for him at his girlfriend's home. Dusty put up with these long drives with me, and I was surprised how strong our bond was growing. My father loved him, and his puppy energy cheered everyone up in a home that had become stifling in some ways from the endless coming and going of hospice nurses and doctors. Dusty would play in the back yard while I gardened for my father, and slowly he started to learn how to bark and trust people. Prior to this, he was so quiet, I just thought he was a dog that didn't bark. Was I wrong about that! Between traveling and the endless assault of new people coming in and out of the home, Dusty went from an introverted, socially aloof puppy to an outgoing ball of joy. He loved everyone!

Of course we adopted him—my first dog ever!—and the Humane Society even paid for the surgery to fix the entropion he had been born with, which caused his eyelid to droop and leak and become irritated.

We decided to name him Apache, because his fur was the dusty-gold of the deserts where the Apache Indians lived. The name seemed to fit for some reason beyond that. I thought of him as a "spirit dog," because he came to me when I felt utterly helpless while caring for my father. Dad lived longer than the doctors had thought was possible with the progression of his cancer. He was not strong enough for treatment, and had been given a two month life expectancy. He lived four months—and Apache was with us through his last days.

Apache gave me no choice but to love him when I felt like I had nothing left to give during the illness. If I were sad, he would curl beside me with his head in my lap, dejected. If I were happy and playing with him, he came alive and rewarded me by coming out of his shell bit by bit over those months. I learned that it was important to be strong for him, because I wanted Apache to be a happy puppy.

Today, Apache is grateful that we do not go in the car too much anymore. He definitely remembers those long rides to Kissimmee each week. He was like a little soldier dog. I feel like we found each other when we both needed the other most. Now, Apache still teaches me lessons about the importance of being strong for him, and he still comes to put his head in my lap when I am a little sad. He loves to shake hands, and will sit by me for a long time while I gently hold his paw and shake it up and down. It relaxes both of us. He is my little spirit dog.

Angel/Lady

Contributed by **Lynda Baker-Sheffer**, Fort Defiance, Virginia

A few years ago, we lost our beloved little Chow, Winnie, a gift to my son, Scott. An angry neighbor put antifreeze in her water bowl while we were out trick or treating on Halloween. Tragically, Winnie died a very painful death. We were all traumatized.

We knew it was important for our family to have another pet. As it happened, an ad appeared in our paper describing a dog named Angel who had undergone terrible experiences and needed love and kindness. She was one of three in the litter who had been penned up in a small cage outdoors that never was cleaned. Her food was thrown on the ground and her water bowl was always dirty.

Her brother at one point escaped the cage but was shot by a neighbor. He survived but was in distress. After that the three pups were taken in by a rescue group, but Angel was the only one available for adoption. We were warned that when we came to visit her in order to see her response to us we should expect her to be so fragile in spirit that she would not allow us to touch her.

We met Angel when she came out for a walk on her leash. My husband Gary took the leash and went a short way. When he stopped so did Angel. Gary asked her, "Do you want to go home with me?" With that she stood up on her hind legs and kissed him squarely on his lips. The decision had been made very clearly by that little dog. She walked with Gary to the truck, and when he opened the door, she went right in and sat in the passenger's seat. Ever since, she has been riding "shotgun."

Angel did not give full trust to our family immediately. It took five years for that. In the beginning we were careful not to make sudden moves near her or cross our legs or feet, and pet her only when she knew that was coming. She follows Gary everywhere, and he renamed her Lady. The only time she barks is when she sees Gary first thing each morning.

An unexplained ability that Angel/Lady has demonstrated involves our daughter April, who is a college student. Lady knows the morning that April will be coming home, and begins to hum! When April comes through the door, Lady is humming, and is joined by April in a loud duet.

For some reason she also likes to visit the Fire Department whenever she has the chance, and spends time with the firemen who happen to be there. Her other favorites are children, cats, and long rides in the truck. Lady also has her own pet—a cat. The two of them play tag and sleep together. Her social life also includes romps with other dogs in our church garden, often acting as the gang leader for a follow-the-leader around the parking lot there.

As for her breed, we comment that she is part Holstein and part Damnation, white with large and small spots on her body. But her real breed is Big Dog with an even bigger heart. Now that she is about twelve or thirteen, she is a little stiff in the mornings but continues to delight in being part of family activities. Although she sleeps a lot more than she used to, she never seems too tired to go somewhere. We hope she will be able to do that for years to come!

Mushkin

Contributed by **Wendy Joseph**, author of *The Witch's Hand*, Wilmington, California

He was the runt of the litter of nine kittens, and after weaning, was so shy he would mush—rhymes with push—himself back into a corner when approached. So Missy at Seattle's Animal Talk rescue gave him to me to foster, because I'm good with the shy ones and can get them to come out and socialize and trust people.

I gave him time, and patience, and named him Mushkin—rhymes with push pin—because of his behavior. Sitting down, I would let my hand drop to where I knew he was crouching, and say without looking at him, "Mommy's hand, see? Just Mommy's hand. It's not going to hurt you." After a while he let Mommy's hand touch him, then pet him gently, then pick him up. He would still mush himself back into my tummy or the crook of my elbow. But he started to trust me and no longer ran when I entered the room.

At night he would curl up beside me, often just under my chin and I would wake up with a mouthful of cat fur. Then he started crawling in under the covers beside me to snuggle up. This is unusual for cats as they don't like having their heads covered up; it's too much like being pounced on by a coyote or other predator going for the throat. But I thought it was sweet that he was so attached to me, and thought seriously of adopting him myself.

I mentioned Mushkin's behavior to Missy and she said it's what cats do when they're sick. Kind of like what I did at five when my appendix fired up and I crawled into bed with my parents so they could make it better. They did. But Mushkin didn't seem sick.

Then he stopped eating. I took him in to the vet for tests, took

103

him home and gave him IV fluids to keep him hydrated. The tests came back positive for Feline Infectious Peritonitis, a hereditary disease that is always fatal. Shocked, I kept him over the weekend to say goodbye. He went downhill before my eyes. He could not eat or relieve himself, and started crawling off into little corners to die. He didn't even want to curl up beside me anymore. It had been ten days since the first symptoms appeared.

Tuesday I put him in the carrier to go to the vet. All the way there, he stared up at me through the openings as if to say, "Where are we going, Mommy? Am I going to feel better there?"

We laid him gently on the table and the vet injected him in the hind leg. I held his head and kept saying, "Mommy's here, Mushkin. Mommy's here." His eyes stayed open, watching me. "He's completely anesthetized," the vet said. She listened through her stethoscope. "There's still a heartbeat." A minute later she listened again, and said, "It's over." He was eight and a half months old.

I could not tell when the life left his body. He was still warm and his eyes were still open. I stayed in the room with him a few more minutes, stroked him, closed his eyes, and cut a bit of his fur off as a remembrance. Then I noticed a yellow trickle slowly moving down the table. He could finally pee.

Goodbye, Mushkin. Take care of him, St. Francis. You look after him now.

Rescue Organizations

The lives of abandoned, neglected, unwanted and mistreated animals are tragic, not only for the animals who suffer, but for those who are guilty of creating those situations. A damaged human psyche harms not only the animals involved but society as a whole. Fortunately for all concerned, there are programs for re-educating human beings about proper care for those who share this earth with them. Especially fortunate for those who suffer are the many rescue organizations, small or private rescue groups, and the work those bodies do to educate the general public as well as provide relief and loving care to the animals.

the eyes
begging or fearful
longing to be free
from pain or hunger

what have they seen
that lingers to haunt
and destroy trust

we offer them new
visions of love
to erase the dark

Patsy

Contributed by **Margaret Underwood**, Greensboro, North Carolina

My dad was an officer in the Navy and stationed in Key West, Florida during World War II. Mother and I moved down there to be with him. I was maybe around nine years old. I was so homesick, missing my friends and familiar places. But there in Florida I used to see a small white dog with loving brown eyes who wandered around our neighborhood. She had medium long fur, but not bushy, and belonged to a woman nearby. The dog was named Patsy and over time she and I bonded deeply.

One day when I went to see Patsy, I couldn't find her, so I asked the woman if she knew where she was. The woman retorted, "I ain't got no time to be chasing after no dog." Long story short, Patsy became our dog. She stuck by me like glue. I also had a pet Rhode Island Red Hen and she and Patsy bonded and even slept together in Patsy's dog house that my dad made. Chick-chick would ride around the yard on Patsy's back. Patsy "de-fleaed" the chicken, nipping her teeth together down to Chick's skin and Chick would spread out while Patsy worked on her, just the way she would do her own skin. Chick ended up soaking wet, of course, so I would dry her off with a towel.

Another one of Patsy's tricks was to bring us a "gift" when we would drive up. She would pick up a nearby stick or a rock. One Thanksgiving she brought us a cut off yellow turkey leg, foot and all, and left it at the front door. She was so proud and seemed to be grinning!

I had to leave for summer camp in Virginia and loved it once I got there. When I returned, Chick, Patsy and I had a joyous reunion. My dad told me that while I was away, Patsy seemed agitated one day, and when he would approach her she would turn away. So my father followed her. He said he felt like a fool, but he followed her about a block away into an open garage that had a grease pit. Chick had fallen down into the pit so Dad fetched her out of it and Patsy was overjoyed.

Soon after I returned from camp Patsy came into heat and every male dog within a mile came "a courting." Patsy had puppies: big ones, way too big for her small body. I heard her in labor, complete with terrible groans and growls, in the dog house which was near my bedroom window. I was too young to understand. I never saw the puppies as my dad took them away … somewhere. He asked me if we should have Patsy "operated on." I said no. He never explained what *kind* of operation, and I had no idea what he meant.

One day as I returned from school on my bike, Patsy did not meet me down the road as usual. I never saw her again. I would wait until my parents were asleep and wander all over Key West looking for her. I went in some terrible neighborhoods, having no idea how dangerous this was. I spent the night with my friend, Ulysse. She and her parents lived close to the Gulf. I thought I heard Patsy barking so off I went in the wee hours of the morning. They soon realized I had gone missing, and found me wandering up and down the beach calling and crying, "Patsy! Patsy!" They told my folks about this but I don't think they were aware of the deep grief I was feeling. I was a very reclusive child and the love I felt for Patsy was the first real love I had ever experienced. She was the love of my life.

We moved back to Greensboro when I was thirteen. When we were driving up to Virginia for my brother's wedding a couple of years later, my dad asked me if I ever wondered what had happened to Patsy and I said yes. Then he told me that I would not let him have her "operated on" so he took her to the pound. I was devastated and cried uncontrollably. He said, "I had no idea that this would hurt you after all this time."

To this day I am not "over" my Patsy. Thinking about how I lost her still brings tearsIf I could choose one animal to join me in Heaven, it would be Patsy.

Clementine

Contributed by **Caroline Carrison,** Greensboro, North Carolina

Clementine called out to me from the pages of a Petfinder ad. She was beautiful and sad.

A professional photographer—Gaynell Parker of Brantley Properties— volunteering her time for a rescue group contributed two photos of her: one perfectly poised in the autumn leaves, her furrowed brow perfectly positioned over the classic droopy-eyed Basset pose. The second photo showed her wearing pearls and looking rather regal as a litter of puppies rolled underneath her, hoping to nurse. Those pictures captivated me for a reason other than her beauty. It was the timing.

My husband and I had just returned from the Thanksgiving holiday, where I had bonded with my sister-in-law's red-boned coonhound, named Clementine. Clementine the coonhound was sweet and calm, and stayed by my side nearly all weekend. I wanted a dog just like her, but condo-sized. I spent the holiday weekend researching dog breeds, and Basset Hounds seemed the perfect match for our lifestyle.

My brother-in-law, who was on the board of his local Humane Society, enjoyed encouraging the search for a dog, but it made my husband concerned that I was taking it all too seriously. He did not want the responsibility of a dog. I came home and began poking around the Petfinder website, wondering if maybe a Basset Hound would appear.

Not a week later, Clementine's picture appeared on the Petfinder website. As I scrolled down to read more about her, my mind began to race as I realized that the rescue group had already named her Clementine. It seemed way too perfect that a Basset Hound showed up bearing the very name of the dog who had inspired my search. Not only that, but the rescue group described her as an "extreme lap dog," so similar to the demeanor of Clementine the coonhound. I was brimming with excitement. It was as if I had torn up a description of the perfect dog into the fireplace and Mary Poppins had arrived. I submitted an application to meet her and waited a few days to tell my husband. Clementine had been with her foster family for a month, recovering from her pre-rescue experiences, when I submitted the application to adopt her. She had been picked up by the rescue group from a rural shelter in eastern North Carolina. Pregnant, emaciated, and heartworm-positive, Clementine had likely been on her own for quite a while. She delivered her puppies after arriving at the rescue shelter. None of them was healthy enough to survive. According to her foster family, she was terribly depressed after the birth. Soon after she delivered, however, a litter of puppies arrived at the rescue without their mom. Clementine was introduced to them and she nursed them as her own. She was treated for heartworms and photographed—wearing pearls!—with her puppies for the rescue website.

My husband really was not pleased with my decision to apply to adopt Clementine. "It's just an application, not a commitment," I told him. I assured him there was really very little chance we would be chosen to adopt her. I knew that rescue groups often required only accepted applicants who lived near or in the town where the rescue group operated. We were an hour and a half away from Clementine. We also lived in a condominium, sure to be a red flag for any rescue organization looking for that perfect patch of grass for their newly rescued souls. She was beautiful and perfect and it was close to Christmas. Someone was bound to see her picture and snatch her up before our application was even given a glance. Logic told me we had a zero chance of getting her.

My heart told me otherwise. This was not a feeling that I have created in hindsight. I proclaimed it to my colleagues at work. I really somehow knew she was our dog. That feeling was there from the beginning.

Despite his general grumpiness about the subject, my husband's gift to me at Christmas was a promise to visit Clementine. He has since confessed that his generosity stemmed from a firm belief that she would already have been adopted. I emailed the rescue organization as soon as we returned from holiday travels, but it had already been several weeks since my application had been submitted. Sure enough, numerous inquiries had come in about Clementine. But my application had been the first to arrive, and the woman at the rescue organization said she was ours if we wanted her.

When we arrived to meet Clementine, she approached me while I was seated on the edge of a brick tree planter. She walked up and sat as close to me as she possibly could. At the time, I believed this was yet another sign that we were put together by some truly other-worldly force. While I still believe that, I now know that her way with me was not necessarily one of those signs. She is like that with everyone, a trusting, quiet, beautiful soul who simply wants to be petted and loved.

My husband made one last effort at thwarting Clementine's adoption by reminding the woman at the rescue that we lived in a condominium. Much to his chagrin, she nonchalantly said, "Well, that's fine. I really don't think Clementine likes to be outside." She added that we needed to purchase soft bedding, as Clementine had grown accustomed to long naps by the window in her foster home. She was ready to live a pampered life.

My husband threw up his hands, and into the car she went.

We have had Clementine for almost three years now. Whatever is in her past seems to have been quietly overcome. It may indeed have been bad. Her front teeth, top and bottom, are brown nubs that sit flush with her gums. The vet suspects that in her former life, she may have worn them down trying to chew through something that was containing her. That is so hard to believe. Her way with humans is so trusting and sweet. She has never shown any interest in chewing anything in our house, ever. I am perplexed by the condition of her teeth and what they must represent about her past.

We have had many laughs about her, like the time she

consumed six bagels at one time and her belly literally swelled to more than twice its size, or when she escaped undetected from the mountain house, was gone for over an hour, and turned up fifty feet away after a frantic search party of five spread over several miles to find her. I must admit, it took me a while to laugh about that escapade. My husband says she looks a bit like a hippo from behind. We laugh when she runs, ears flopping in the wind with her hippo-bottom swaying from side to side.

She could win sleeping awards. Before our son was born, Clementine was the best couch sleeper anyone could ask for. She would cozy up next to me in the tightest spot possible and really snore it out. I did not know a dog could sleep twenty-two hours out of nearly every day.

She remains the best cuddler, too. If I sit down on the floor, she is next to me in an instant, rolled over for a snuggle and a belly rub. She will stay there as long as I am there.

For a dog who was severely underweight when she was found, she is the least food-motivated dog I have ever met. While she never misses a meal or a dropped morsel from the high chair, she does not let food interfere with her will to be stubborn. It is impossible to use a treat to get her to do anything she does not want to do. In the mornings before work, if she has already curled up into her bed, she will not, under any circumstances, move to her crate—which looks equally soft and inviting in my eyes, by the way. No amount of ham or turkey-flavored dog treats will get her to move. She can actually make herself heavier if she wants to stay put. I have spent countless mornings dragging Clementine, in her bed, to the crate opening and nudging her into the crate. She loves her crate on her own terms, but if she is already comfortable somewhere else, a Thanksgiving feast would not motivate her to move.

She is temperature sensitive. She hates air conditioning vents and waits before bed so her blanket can be positioned over her. Last summer, she stopped during a walk because she was hot and refused to move. My husband had to come pick us up in the car. Some neighbors recently commented that they have never met a rescue dog who acted so ladylike and confident. They find it humorous that our rescue dog acts so completely *debonaire*, as if she has forgotten her roots "on the street."

The most striking thing about Clementine, however, is the joy that she brings daily to everyone she meets. My husband calls her "Lady Wagsalot." We live in the downtown area, so she passes many people every day on her walks. It is amazing to witness the joy she brings. People of all walks of life, all races, colors, ages, and stations, stop to say something about Clementine. Her many different attributes become topics of conversation: Her beauty, her basset-ness, her likeness to television dogs—"That's the Dukes of Hazard dog!"—her most-of-the-time good manners on the leash. I love passing people in the park and watching them follow her with their eyes before they comment on her. I frequently smile to myself when someone says, upon receiving a greeting from Clementine, "Oh, she must know I love dogs." The truth is she treats everyone that way. When a hand reaches down to pet her, her tail folds under and she flops onto her back, asking for a belly rub.

After a scary trip to the vet, which thankfully turned out to be nothing serious, my boss reminded me that having a dog "really is a love affair." The fullness I feel in my heart when I am with her could only be described as the feeling of complete and utter love and adoration. She completes me.

115

Rocky

Contributed by **Yvonne Kratz**, Wilson, North Carolina

One day while looking at pictures of dogs on my computer, my daily practice, I saw a little shelter dog who tugged at my heart. Even though I had two dogs and was not in the market for another, I kept going back to that picture all day long. A message was later posted that the little fellow was to be put to sleep the following day. My heart sank.

He was a Shih Tzu, but nothing to look at, by his picture, his little head hanging down. I could see the fur growing over his eyes, and the sad expression that covered his face. I knew with a strong intuitiveness that this little dog needed me, and also that I needed him. We needed each other! So I drove the fifty miles to where he was, and I am so glad that I did. The lady at the shelter told me that someone brought him in and just walked away. He was so thin his backbone looked like the blade on an ice skate. The probable story was that his owner had died and her family did not want to keep him.

As soon as I held him, my feelings were confirmed that we had to be together. I noticed that his front paw appeared either to have been broken or that he had a birth defect. In spite of learning that his dry eyes would require expensive drops daily, and seeing that he badly needed grooming, I knew that under all that fur was a heart of gold and a loving bundle of doggie. I adopted him that day.

My first stop on the way home was our vet, where he was checked out, and then Rocky, his new name, came home to meet Ginger and Mugsy Baja, my other two dogs. The three of them

117

immediately bonded, playing as if they had always been together. Despite his crippled front paw, he soon was able to outrun the other dogs. Rocky fit right into our household routine.

I had heard that a rescued dog appreciates everything we can do for him, and this is true of Rocky. He is the most loving little fellow I have ever seen, and will lie in my arms sleeping like a baby. My family is now complete, with my two Shih Tzus and the Golden Retriever.

The Humane Society of the United States

The Humane Society of the United States, HSUS, is the nation's largest animal protection organization, with the support of eleven million Americans.

Their work includes advocating for better laws protecting animals; campaigns to reform industries involving animals; animal rescue and emergency response; investigation of animal cruelty; and caring for animals through their sanctuaries and wildlife rehabilitation centers, emergency shelters and clinics.

Operating for more than fifty years, The HSUS is not related to local animal shelters, but is a strong advocate for adoption from shelters and rescue groups.

The HSUS was established as a national advocacy organization to do the kinds of work, and help animals, that generally fall outside the scope of local animal groups. Their goal is to reduce suffering and to create meaningful social change for animals.

Faith

Contributed by **Patsy Beeker**, Concord, North Carolina

What good is one more human being when you're dying? Ask Faith. She would have died last night, when the temperatures dropped below freezing and she had no shelter except for the shallow hole she had pawed in the mud to lie in so that the wind didn't pelt her bony frame. The humans Faith knew hadn't done much good for her.

She didn't know why they no longer wanted her to live. She didn't understand why they took down her kennel and tied her on a six-foot chain outside the back door of the house, with no shelter or bedding, not even a tree overhead. And she couldn't figure out why they stopped feeding her, unless they just wanted her to die.

It wouldn't take long now. Faith had endured torrential rains for two days and the northeastern wind that blasted in the first freezing cold front of November. She couldn't remember when she last ate, but it had been days. Her only water came from the skies, when she looked up and whimpered and it ran between her slack lips.

But then one person helped her. One sympathetic neighbor couldn't stand to watch any longer and called an animal hotline. The neighbor took time to explain how serious the situation was.

Faith didn't have much time. The woman who answered the telephone call didn't have much time, either. On a beautiful Saturday afternoon, there were yard chores to do and errands to run, and her husband was about to leave on a business trip. But she was the only one who could investigate the call that weekend.

So she called her husband and she called a friend, one good friend who was always willing to bring along a camera to document the story of an animal's suffering. Daylight was rapidly fading when they drove far out into the country to look for the address where Faith was dying. What good could they do, these humans who had good intentions but knew the limits of the law that prohibited them from taking Faith away from that awful place?

They found the house, and they recognized it immediately because surely nobody else would have starved and abused a dog like those in the house where Faith lived. In fact, they didn't even find the dog until she raised her head wearily and the people saw that the muddy bundle in the earth was a fully-grown Doberman Pinscher.

They fed her and gave her water and rubbed her head gently. But that was all they could do for her, because the dog's owners either were away or would not answer the pounding on their door. So they left a note and went home, and Faith settled down again with her bony rump turned into the wind as darkness fell around her.

Monday was a holiday. The neighbor who called in the report waited for authorities to arrive. The woman who drove out into the night to look for the starving dog also waited. The friend who went with her waited. But it was a long drive, and holidays meant only a skeleton staff to investigate all the calls in the whole county where too many dogs had no shelter and strays roamed country roads looking for new homes. There wasn't enough time to send an authority to check on all the animals. So the day passed, and the next day was busy catching up. After all, Faith was only one dog in a county where many animals suffered.

By Wednesday, her time was running out. The previous day had dumped over an inch of rain on her. When the clouds blew away, bitter chill settled in. Temperatures that night would be in the low thirties. And Faith had nothing between her and cold air, and no fat left on her body to protect her. Her spine protruded, her ribs stuck out, and from the rear her pelvis looked like an anatomy drawing of the skeleton of a dog. Open sores on her hip bones ached miserably. The distance between her hips measured about four inches, with most of the muscle tissue of her body devoured by starvation. The authorities came that afternoon, but again no one answered the door. By law they had to leave a warning and come back the next day. It would be too late by then.

Faith heard one more car pull into her driveway. One lady hadn't given up on her, and one animal rescuer couldn't get that image out of her mind. Together they had come out in late afternoon to be sure the Doberman was fed. The rescuer was a petite blonde, a soft-spoken, gentle little woman with more strength in her soul than a Sumo wrestler. Her friend was equally mild-mannered and polite. You wouldn't suspect either of them fighting for the last piece of chocolate cake, much less for a dog. Together they drove at night into a neighborhood that tough policemen often feared and pounded on the door of a man who was no stranger to the law, knowing that all around them hostile eyes watched behind doors and windows to see what would happen next. He answered and he was angry.

Unknown to them, two guardian angel deputies watched from a short distance away to protect them from harm. But the deputies did not need to fear evil. The woman spoke her mind, and in a few minutes the dog owner signed a release allowing her to take Faith away. They slipped a leash on the Doberman, and she almost dragged them to the car, as though she knew it was her last chance for survival. Faith settled down on the floor and sighed and closed her eyes on the way to the veterinary clinic. After a quick checkup, the vet confirmed that she would not have lived through the night. They bundled her into a warm bed, fed her, and hoped that she'd make it until morning.

Less than twenty-four hours later the women came back to visit, and Faith was already a different animal. When the clinic workers bathed her, she swayed under the warm shower and seemed to know that they were helping her. Mud and dead hair swirled down the drain. When she dried and went to the exercise pen, the dog who was so weak she could barely lift her head frisked and played. Not gracefully, and not for long, but her face radiated joy that she had been saved. She posed for more photos to document her condition and snuggled against the arms of those who took care of her. Not one person, but a group of caring people who would be sure she never went hungry again.

So what good did one person do to save the life of this dog?

One reached out to another, who called another to help, who phoned others, who added vets and staff workers and an entire community of animal lovers to end the suffering of one creature. But it had to start with one. Her name isn't really Faith. She doesn't seem to know her given name, as though she's had so little contact with people that it just doesn't mean much to her. But she is the personification of faith, the faith that if one person comes forward, others will follow. The faith that even though all suffering animals can't be rescued, the one who is saved will make it worthwhile. The faith that one person can perform a miracle and make a mountain from a mud pile.

millions of lost, abandoned,
abused beyond belief—
other millions of homes open
to welcome the rejected,
offer a new life of safety
from former dangers
and terrors of the night—
caresses and food combine
to feed hungry spirits
nourish them to health
by care and love
by kindness beyond necessity

125

Tig & Bumble

Contributed by **Martha Orrick Milot**, Jamestown, Rhode Island

Tig is our "cruisin' kitty". He came from an animal rescue center in Rhode Island. He is our third rescue cat, acquired at age two. We suspect that he was abused by a male in the household from which he came. The abuse must have included the use of a broom or stick. Even if I pick up a yard stick he runs.

He has become my best buddy and follows me everywhere. While I type he sits on my lap, but he is wary of my husband Arthur. That is sad because Art loves all animals, and cats in particular. As a volunteer for the Potter Animal Rescue League, a state of the art rescue home, Art would take cats they could not place and keep them in his office until they were socialized. Then he'd return them to Potter for adoption. Now, after nine years with us, Tig has begun to appreciate Art.

We know that Tig is a very smart cat. If he wants a treat he bangs with both front paws on the cabinet, both on the boat and at home. We spend much of our time on our boat, and he has traveled with us from Maine to Florida. Does he like it? I think yes, as long as the engine is not running. When we are underway he spends his time in the pilot house in his bed and behind pillows. I sit next to him, with Art next to me. When we turn off the engine his exploring resumes. Tig is an indoor cat on land, but when we anchor when we are on the boat, he enjoys the run of the deck looking at birds, although a pelican on the bow made him run for cover, and seems fascinated by the motion of the water.

We had an interesting moment once when we were anchored in Florida. Tig was swatting at a bug, and lost his balance and fell into the water. Art saw what happened and jumped in after Tig — with his glasses on. The glasses went to the bottom of the briny

127

deep. Then he called to me to hand him the net we keep aboard so that he could fish Tig out of the water. But he dropped the net, which joined his glasses. Tig then began swimming like crazy. Art swam after him, of course. When Tig spied him, Tig climbed onto Art's head and clung on with his claws! Fortunately a dinghy approached and Art called out, emphasizing each word: "Please. Get. Cat. Off. My. Head!"

The owner of the dinghy complied and passed Tig over to me on the boat. Art then climbed aboard, his face covered with blood. Just another day in the life with our Tig!

As a postscript, I'll add that our grandson carries on the family tradition of rescuing animals. When he was nine, he found an Alaskan Malamute at the local shelter, and my son agreed to take

him home. They named him Bumble. He had been picked up by the animal control officers who had been notified that the dog was tied night and day to a tree. My son also has rescued cats, one from the Potter Animal Rescue League, and a kitten found by the side of the

road. We have believed that animals deserve to treated with loving care and none should end their lives abandoned, abused, or neglected.

(Note : Before his story could be published, Tig crossed the Rainbow Bridge to a new life. But Artie, the new feline sailor, also from the Potter Animal Rescue League, is preparing to take his first cruise very soon.)

Glenwood

As told to the author by Alan Brilliant, Greensboro, North Carolina

Alan Brilliant owns a small bookstore known as Glenwood Coffee and Books near the University of North Carolina at Greensboro. One day while his friend Joseph was working on a house in the area, he found a kitten who appeared to be about a week old, and took him in. He was unable to find the mother, so he began feeding it according to what he thought a kitten needed for proper nourishment.

Joseph had a girl friend in Florida whom he visited from time to time, and he asked Al to keep the kitten while he was away. "Only for a week," Joseph begged. So Al agreed to be the caretaker. A problem arose, however, when Joseph returned to claim his new pet. By that time Al had become very attached to the little creature, as had many of his customers. He refused to give him up to Joseph. Joseph reluctantly agreed, and the kitten now makes his home with Al, who lives in one part of the book store.

Then the customers said the kitten needed a name, so they held a contest on the bookstore's Facebook page: "Name the Cat." Al's preference was Gus, short for Asparagus, but the main preference among the Facebook entries was that the kitten should be named Glenwood. After all, he is the permanent resident of Glenwood Coffee and Books!

Glenwood grows rapidly, and Al has to teach him safety lessons, especially about not running into the street. Blocking his attempts with a broom seems to work so far. Glenwood is learning very quickly how to socialize with the bookstore customers, all the while keeping an eye out for any restrictions that might be imposed upon his wanderings. Soon he will probably begin to read, or at least listen while Al reads stories to him. After all, Glenwood is bound to be a book lover, because he is surrounded by wonderful books!

Morris Animal Foundation

Dedicated to improving the health of animals, the Morris Animal Foundation was established in 1948 by Dr. Mark L. Morris, Sr. He was one of the first veterinarians to control animal disease by use of correct diet. Buddy was a Seeing Eye guide dog owned by Morris Frank, national ambassador for the Seeing Eye organization. Brought by Frank to Dr. Morris to be treated for kidney failure, Buddy was the first to benefit from a special diet created to improve his condition. Soon more requests for the diet came in, which originally was made and canned in the Morris' home kitchen. Eventually they partnered with a packing company to produce Hill's Pet Nutrition Prescription Diet. From the royalties of those early sales the Morris Animal Foundation was established, funding research into nutrition for dogs and cats.

The resulting achievements of that early effort to treat Buddy have grown to include humane animal health studies in institutions, veterinary medicine colleges, and zoos. Nearly thirty student projects at veterinary schools are also funded by the Foundation.

Buddy was not only a guide for the visually impaired, but he became the catalyst for a thriving organization that attends to the needs of animal health.

Sully

Contributed by **Patsy Beeker**, Concord, North Carolina

Since 2005, my dog Sully has visited with thousands of school children, Boy and Girl Scouts and pre-schoolers all over North Carolina. He has been our "ambassador" to teach these children about how to care for pets, to keep them safe, and to be responsible for their well-being. In the first year of our program, we counted how many little folks we met. At the end of that year, we had met with slightly over 1300, and we stopped counting. The program snowballed after that. From September until May, the regular school calendar, Sully sees an average of two groups each week, traveling as far as fifty or sixty miles over five counties in the state.

It wasn't the life that was intended for him. He was supposed to die. When Sully was about six weeks old, he and his brother were delivered to the local Animal Shelter to be euthanized. They were unwanted, unplanned pups. Instead, they were chosen for the Humane Society's dog adoption program. Often, I see a dog that looks very similar in size or conformation and I wonder if there's a relationship to this odd-looking little guy. But I've never seen quite the same combination. He has a barrel chest and short, bowed legs. His head is a bit small for his body, and his spine is a tad longer than it should be. The set of his tail and ears are somewhat "Beagle-ish," but his brindle coloring indicates boxer or pit bull heritage. His face could be any of a number of toy breeds. He looks like he'd weigh in at about twenty-five pounds, and vets are always surprised when he tips the scales at forty. He's a solid little chunk of muscle. And when he wags his tail and smiles his peculiar little welcome to children, he's forty pounds of joy. Kids can't resist him. Few have skipped the chance to rub his head or his tummy, even those who first hopped up on chairs or desks in fear when a dog walked into the classroom.

In our presentations, we go over the basics: how to greet a strange dog, what to do if you are attacked by a dog, and the warning not to tease a dog on a chain or in a kennel. When I tell them they shouldn't startle a sleeping dog, Sully obligingly rolls on his side and feigns naptime. We say that any dog who has teeth can bite, and he curls his lips to look fierce. I advise them to be like a turtle if attacked; a turtle pulls his head and limbs into a shell. The children curl into little balls on the floor and Sully sniffs around them to see if a vulnerable face or neck might be licked. They giggle as he sniffs and tickles their backs. He's quite the teacher, Sully is.

I think about a class of special needs students we visited last spring. A little girl with funny glasses and severe disabilities shrieked and ran away when she saw the dog. She hid behind her desk and cried. Sully kept throwing her glances, flirting and wagging his tail until he won her over. Twenty minutes later she sat on the floor and hugged him. "I love you, Sully," she said. "I think you love me, too. I know you do."

One of my favorite memories is a small rural school where a little girl with profound disabilities scuttled in a half-crawl around the room. Her eyes were set far apart on her face so that she turned from side to side to watch him. Other children in wheelchairs and walkers surrounded him, squealing and pumping him with awkward rubs. The teacher watched the little girl. "She never responds to anything we do," she said. Sully smiled and wagged his tail slowly at her. She rolled to one side of him and studied him, then rolled in a semi-circle in the other direction. Sully stepped forward and licked her ever so gently on the temple, a sweet little doggie-kiss on her forehead. She giggled and a huge grin appeared. The teacher had tears rolling down her face. "I've never seen her smile."

That's what he does best. He makes children and adults smile and want to love him. It's his gift.

I have photos and memories of him in nursing homes, getting

134

kisses from plump little women slumped in wheelchairs. I remember autistic children in wheelchairs and headgear, watching for his signals, welcoming him into their laps and smiling. I remember so many tearful parents who saw their children respond in unusual ways to his wet nose nuzzling them. It is possible that in some unfathomable way, he communicates to them, "I understand, I wasn't perfect either, I wasn't supposed to live. But here I am."

In eight years, he's touched a lot of lives.

intimate caregiver
receiving the lost
abandoned and injured
no measure for time
spent nor for cost
applied to lives unlike
our own, we who have
no feathers or extra paws
no strength to carry riders
no hunger for field grass
we are not raptors nor deer
but merely creature partners
while the Vet
tends with care all the ones
great and small and gives them
what the rest of us cannot do
a holy calling

Dogs at Home

Our family has had many dogs, some purchased, others who just showed up. Here are descriptions of a few of them, mostly those who "happened" into our yard.

My first dog was a black Cocker Spaniel with the unremarkable name of Inky. My parents really didn't want more dogs to care for. They'd had several during the years before I was born, when my older brothers were growing up. I was fourteen, and we lived in Army quarters at Fort Lewis, Washington. One of my friends told me they had one puppy left from a litter and had not been able to find a home for her. When I went to see her, that was enough for me and I walked her home. My concerns about my father telling me we couldn't have another dog were soon eased when he saw us coming and greeted the little dog I led by a leash, "Well, hello, little girl." For the rest of her long life, Inky was spoiled by my mother and given many little treats by my stern father the Army doctor. She lived to be thirteen, and was a wonderful companion to my parents when I married and spent three years in Germany with my husband while he served his commitment to the Air Force in Bremerhaven. She greeted us upon our return, even though we brought with us our two-year-old daughter who loved to chase Inky through the house, much to the old dog's displeasure. A few years later she breathed her last, peacefully, with my parents at her side.

Many dogs and a couple of cats followed in our own family, but none came from shelters. A few were dogs who showed up in our yard, letting us know they wanted to live with us, but we have no idea what the stories were that sent them out on their own, seeking new homes. We had many breeds, some thoroughbred and others of mixed parentage. Our canine companions lived long, pleasant lives with us until old age left them unable to keep going.

Heidi

When my husband and I settled in the town of Madison, North Carolina after our time with the Air Force in Bremerhaven, Germany, we were a family of three, with our two-year-old Kit. It was time to begin our family of pets. Our first one was Heidi, a Chihuahua-Terrier mix. She was not a rescued dog but instead was chosen for her size and suitability for Kit to learn the care of pets. Little did we know that some decades years later she would be caring for a household of Chihuahuas or blends thereof, rescued from various situations. Bebe, our cover girl for this book, is one of those.

Brownie

For a time, we rented a small house on a busy road. A caramel-colored dog would come to our yard often, although we thought he was from another home across the road from us. We were not looking for another pet at that time. We had plans for the home we would build on a mountain ridge next door to good friends, which would be a far better place for any pets than our current location with its dangerous traffic, and were waiting for the completion of that house. But the dog from across the road began coming frequently to our house. Eventually, we decided to feed him, and, of course, he did indeed become our dog. We named him— appropriately—Brownie. He would roam, however, and one time had a fierce encounter with some other dogs, limping home with many wounds. The vet gave us medicine to treat his injuries and he survived that agony. When we finally moved into our new home on the "mountain" he came with us.

Brownie was a wonderful companion for us and for our children. One day he came down the long drive to our place with his new girlfriend, a black and white dog who seemed friendly enough. But we didn't believe we could take in another dog at that time and gave her to some friends who lived in Madison, the town below us. They named her Blackie. Not long after that, we got a call from our friends notifying us that Blackie was pregnant, and must have been when our dog brought her home, because she was almost due. Blackie's pups were adorable and all found homes quickly. One went to a home near where we would be living after we sold our mountain home in order to be closer to school and the town events. Blackie spent the rest of her life with our friends and was happy.

While we still lived on the "mountain," Brownie disappeared one Easter weekend when we were out of town. We never learned what happened to him.

Winston

I seem to be the only one in our family who believes this, but the little dog who some years later wandered into our yard in Madison

where we had moved a few years before, was a descendant of our Brownie. It seems that an offspring of Blackie, who lived in town, had fathered the little pup. As what I consider certain proof, not long after that dog appeared, whom we named Winston, a female pup showed up, just like Winston except for being black and white, whereas Winston was caramel and white. Same markings, same kind of voice, same size. We were certain she was Winston's sister, and we found a good home for her. Their father was a neighborhood Romeo, we were told. So to this day I am certain that our dear Brownie was Winston's grandfather.

Winston lived seventeen years, and was a smart and friendly member of our family who got along well with our other dogs. His one unbreakable habit was to dig out from under the fenced pen in our back yard and take our other two dogs with him to go exploring downtown. Fortunately, they were never hurt before I could find them and bring them back home. A few months before Winston died, however, he managed to slip away one night when he was let out in the front yard instead of in the dog lot. Several days later, someone found him around midnight starting across the bridge that led out of town. Because he was almost completely deaf and blind by then, it is really a miracle he survived. A neighbor happened along and took Winston back toward our house, believing he might belong to us or to another family on our street. The next morning, our next door neighbor, my husband's brother, saw Winston slipping through the hedge to our house and went over to let him inside. Winston lived several more months, ultimately dying at home.

Murphey

One afternoon a strange dog wandered into our yard. A mix of tan and dark brown fur, her front and back ends seemed to belong to two different dogs. We used to say that she looked as though she were put together by a committee. We decided that was one dog too many for us, though, and ignored her. The following day our son heard a great commotion of barking dogs down the hill from us, where the town ran its waste treatment plant. Stray dogs were kept there temporarily. He went down to investigate and found a number of dogs, with one halfway under the fence and another trying to pull him back by his tail. And in that company was the dog who had showed up at our place. He reported back to us, but we did not act on that information, hoping that somehow the local vet, who would be receiving these dogs soon and would hold them for a few days, would find a home for the dog. By that time we knew she was a female.

Guess who showed up the next day in our garage? We called her to us. My husband happened to be around as well. "No more dogs," he said in exasperation. And then he looked at her. "Don't show it to me again. You two make the decision. My son and I looked at each other, put the dog in our car, and off to the vet's we went for a checkup, shots and whatever else might be needed to get the newcomer cleared for living with us. On the way, we

142

passed Murphey Street, named for a founder of our town, and I said, "That's what we'll name her: Murphey."

We did make one attempt to find a good home for her, but the family who took her returned her, saying she barked and barked at their parakeet and they could not take her after all. So Murphey became our dog. She had little to offer us in return but loyalty, permission to love her as much as we could, and the need to lick our toes.

She did get into some scrapes along the way. She returned home one afternoon so covered with river mud that all we could see were two eyes and a nose. It took over an hour to clean her up. Another time she and Winston went under our house, through the crawl space, after some critter, and Murphey was afraid to come back out. My husband had to crawl to her, under the full length of the house the next morning, past various dead rodents along the way. The entrances to the crawl spaces were barred from that day forward. A day or so later we discovered an act of bravery Murphey had performed while under our house when the strong smell of dead snake came wafting through our heating vents.

She loved to dig out under the dog lot fence with Winston and our Westie, Zelda Fitzgerald, to roam the town, and became quite expert at getting through any fenced area we had around our yard. But she survived all her escapades, lived to be about thirteen, and died peacefully at home. She had a good life.

Willie and Katie

Even though they are not rescued animals, I can't omit our last two dogs, Willie and Katie. Willie, a black Lab and son of our Raney, a chocolate Lab, has gone on to his new existence, but he and Katie were good friends for the few years they were together. He was a mama's boy, and dependent on Raney for instructions, so when she died, he struggled to find his own path. We moved a year or so

143

later and he adjusted well to our new home. His only fear was thunder. He could not be consoled during a storm, but stayed close to us for protection. When Katie, a Beagle-Jack Russell, joined us, the two found companionship. He was like a big brother to her. The day he left us, Katie and I spent most of the afternoon beside him as he lay on the rug in our bedroom. When the veterinarian and her helpers arrived, he wagged his tail in greeting but could not get up. By then his back and hips no longer could bear his weight, as slight as it had become. His final journey was a gentle one, and I believe he has found lasting joy.

Katie is now sole manager of our household, and commands with her sharp Beagle bark, often to our distress. She makes commentary on all that takes place in our neighborhood, and is a social animal. Whenever our children stop by, especially when they bring their own dogs, Katie is a blur of excitement and little yips. We hope she will be with us for a long time yet.

A Not-So-Final Word

The stories, the articles about rescue organizations and animal care foundations that are shared here do not end the need for telling about the lives of animals. They live with us, in shelters, on the streets, in the wilds, in zoos, in their native habitats. Each creature on our planet has value in some way for the continuation of life for all.

There are situations where decisions must be made as to what is best for the greatest number of us, what makes for a sustainable environment, and what is necessary for life to exist. These situations do not have real meaning, however, without a sense of human compassion, that ingredient required of all of us in order to survive and have a worthwhile existence.

There are no solutions in these pages for how such a goal is achieved. We must make painful decisions. We must consider the lilies, so to speak, and realize that all that is here is a gift to be tended as it was created to be.

Yet beyond our efforts there is a universal sense that somehow the possibilities will present what is needed if only we remain open to perceiving them. We can learn what must be done to afford life in its fullness for all that lives, whether it is an ant, a dolphin or an elephant, a lemur or a beloved family pet.

We are at the moment in history where we must recognize the necessity for such life or suffer the consequences if we fail to care for what ultimately will sustain us.

If what you have read in these pages touches you enough to desire more for all our lives, then you know there is work calling out to be accomplished. The time will not always be given us to provide what is needed for all of life. Let us begin.

Some Rescue Organization Contact Info

National Organizations:

American Society for the Prevention of Cruelty to Animals®
424 E. 92nd Street; New York, New York 10128-6804; 212-876-7700
www. aspca.org

Cinderella Pet Rescue Organization
P.O. Box 533; Penitas, TX 78576; 956-391-4399
www.cinderella-pet-rescue.org

The Humane Society of the United States
2100 L Street, NW; Washington, DC 20037; 202-452-1100
www.humanesociety.org

Morris Animal Foundation
10200 East Girard Ave., Suite B430; Denver, CO 80231; 800-243-2345; 303-790-2345
mailbox@MorrisAnimalFoundation.org

A Few North Carolina Rescue and Foster Groups, and Shelters in Guilford County

Animal Rescue and Foster Program
Post Office Box 77393; Greensboro, NC 27417; 336-574-9600
www.arfpnc.com

Guilford County Animal Shelter
4525 W. Wendover Avenue; Greensboro, NC 27409; 336-297-5020
Post Office Box 8; Jamestown, NC 27282
www.adoptshelterpets.org   Susie's Law: Facebook

Red Dog Farm – Animal Rescue Network
(Mail): 5803 Bur-Mil Club Road (Actual): 5836 Bur-Mil Club Road
Greensboro, NC 27410; 336-644-7807

www.reddogfarm.com   reddogfarm@triad.rr.com

In addition:
Cabarrus CARES – Kitty City
36 Union Street, Concord, NC 28025; 704-795-5219
www.kittycityconcord.org

About the Author

Jean Rodenbough grew up loving animals of all kinds. Later, she wrote stories about animals and people, poems about everything, and trained for several different careers.

She is a retired Presbyterian minister, serving mostly as a chaplain with hospice and with hospitals. She also has taught both English and ethics in secondary school and college. She earned several degrees in the process: BA, MA, M.Div., and D.Min, but her focus now is on her writing of both poetry and prose.

This book is her second with All Things That Matter, the first one *Rachel's Children: Surviving the Second World War.*

She and her husband Charles live in Greensboro, North Carolina.

ALL THINGS THAT MATTER PRESS ™

FOR MORE INFORMATION ON TITLES AVAILABLE FROM
ALL THINGS THAT MATTER PRESS, GO TO
http://allthingsthatmatterpress.com
or contact us at
allthingsthatmatterpress@gmail.com

Made in the USA
Charleston, SC
18 December 2012